Also by Chris Rodell

Fiction
Evan & Elle in Heaven & Hell:
A Long-Distance Social Media Afterlife Love Story
2020

The Last Baby Boomer:
The Story of the Ultimate Ghoul Pool
2017

Nonfiction
Arnold Palmer:
Homespun Stories of The King
2018

Hole in One!
The Complete Book of Fact, Legend, and
Lore on Golf's Luckiest Shot
2003

Chris blogs at ...

www.EightDaysToAmish.com

Growing Up in Mister Rogers' REAL Neighborhood

: Life Lessons from The Heart of Latrobe, PA

CHRIS RODELL

 iUniverse®

GROWING UP IN MISTER ROGERS'
REAL NEIGHBORHOOD
: LIFE LESSONS FROM THE HEART OF LATROBE, PA

iUniverse books may be ordered through booksellers or by contacting:

iUniverse
1663 Liberty Drive
Bloomington, IN 47403
www.iuniverse.com
1-800-Authors (1-800-288-4677)

Scripture quotations from the Holy Bible, King James Version (Authorized Version). First published in 1611. Quoted from the KJV Classic Reference Bible.

ISBN: 978-1-5320-8083-8 (sc)
ISBN: 978-1-5320-8084-5 (e)

Library of Congress Control Number: 2019912548

Print information available on the last page.

iUniverse rev. date: 09/10/2019

For being one of those guys who "got" me before he even met me, this book is dedicated to Shaughnessy Bishop-Stall. When guys like you believe in guys like me, we begin to believe it's okay to begin believing in ourselves.

Contents

Preface xi

Foreword xv

Author's Note on Profanity xvii

Chapter 1   America's Least Likely Superhero.................... 1

Chapter 2   Gandhi, MLK ... & Fred Rogers? 7

Chapter 3   Is Latrobe Truly Special? 13

     Life Lesson: Our Neighborhood Opioid crisis 21

Chapter 4   Relevant Landmarks................................. 25

     Life Lesson: Crowded Funerals............................ 33

Chapter 5   I was 'Born' in Latrobe 35

Chapter 6   Colorful Neighbors 41

Chapter 7   Were Arnold & Fred Pals? 47

     Life Lesson: Friendship................................. 51

Chapter 8   Monuments to Fred................................. 53

Chapter 9   Fred's Hero....................................... 59

     Life Lesson: Bullying................................. 62

Chapter 10 Joy Riding the Idlewild Trolley 67

     Life Lesson: Fatherhood 71

Chapter 11 Lah-Trobe or LAYtrobe? 75

Chapter 12 Good Deeds 81

     Life Lesson: Waking Up Determined to do Good ...83
     Life Lesson: Good Deeds at the Dry Cleaner 86
     Life Lesson: WWJD about Latrobe's
     Homeless Dude (and What I Did)..........................89

Chapter 13 Married by Mr. Rogers..93

Chapter 14 When You're in no Mood to See People &
     You See Fred Rogers 99

     Life Lesson: Making Bad Days Better 103

Chapter 15 Latrobe: A Land of Legends 107

     Legend I: So what was Arnold Palmer Really Like? ...108
     Legend II: The History of the 1st Banana Split
     & Bank Robbery Festival 111
     Legend III: Stop Drinking Rolling Rock! It's
     Made in New Jersey 113
     Legend IV: Lambs, Latrobe & Dr. Lechter........... 118

Chapter 16 Politics.. 121

     Life Lesson: Being Undecided 128

Chapter 17 Death 131

     Life Lesson: Small-Town Funeral Etiquette 134
     Life Lesson: Dow Carnahan The Voice of Latrobe....136
     Life Lesson: Excessive Mourning.......................... 139
     Life Lesson: Death of the World's Most
     Cheerful Man.. 142

Chapter 18 Happiness... 145

        Life Lesson: Doin' Time... 153
        Life Lesson: Time.. 157

Chapter 19 Being Diagnosed with an Incurable Disease 159

        Life Lesson: Latrobe's best hugger 164
        Life Lesson: The Will to Live................................. 166

Chapter 20 Comparing Fred to Jesus 171

        Life Lesson: J-Students Quizzing Christ................. 176

Chapter 21 I Finally Meet Mr. Rogers; It Does Not Go Well 179

        Life Lesson: Drug-Addicted Babies........................ 188

Chapter 22 Giving a High School Commencement in
        Mister Rogers' REAL Neighborhood 191

Chapter 23 Trolley Magic 195

Acknowledgements 199

Preface

When I began blogging about life in a small town back in 2008 many of my well-meaning friends in the publishing industry advised me of the need to, as one put it, "cultivate a niche" (he pronounced it NEE-shay.).

"The only way to succeed is by concentrating on some narrow topic," he said. "You could be Cigar Guy!"

I told him I didn't want to be Cigar Guy. My smoke-averse wife and daughters would insist I simultaneously become Lives-In-The-Woods Guy.

"Well, what kind of guy do you want to be?"

I told him I'd be content being Latrobe Guy. There's plenty of good company in that humble designation. I told him my intention was to write about what it was like to live in a small western Pennsylvania town, pop. 7,949.

"Nothing ever happens in towns like that."

I said I believed my unique circumstances meant this could be one of those rare instances where a whole lot of nothing could really add up to something. I couldn't explain it — still can't — but there's just something about Latrobe. I've since then written more than 2,000 posts mostly about the town where nothing happens.

You may have heard of it. It is the birthplace of both Fred Rogers and Arnold Palmer. The town also cradled Rolling Rock beer, the banana split and professional football. Each summer tens of thousands of Pittsburgh Steeler fans come to Latrobe to watch the Pittsburgh Steelers practice at scenic Saint Vincent College.

Travel Channel in '18 named Latrobe one of the 50 most charming towns in America, one year after Smithsonian Magazine declared us one of the 20 small towns to visit.

That's plenty to write about right there. In between, I'd write about my family, recreation, the restaurants, local crime, worship and how you're supposed to react if you're in the Giant Eagle and Arnold Palmer asks if you'd like to play the lottery with him (you tell him yes and fork over $20).

It's the kind of town where people often greet one another, not with "Hello" or any of the formal salutations, but with a cheerful, "Hey!"

Yes, everyday in Latrobe is a real heyday!

As it was the inspiration for many of the people, settings and lessons for the iconic show, we're also renowned as the "Real Mister Rogers Neighborhood." Like many of you, he's a foundational role model many of us aspire to emulate.

But it's also a very real neighborhood. There is crime, police standoffs, political division, heartbreak, etc. It's a place where the passing of a regular guy is treated like the death of a king and the death of The King was celebrated because in Latrobe he acted like he was just a regular guy.

It's all been there in the blog, a venue where my goal was to be funny or at least informative. But funny first. Always.

And speaking of funny, a funny thing happened along the way. A blog about a small town where nothing happens began earning a devoted readership from all around the world. I still don't really understand why. I think it's because the blog cast a cheerful eye toward the future, while remaining firmly rooted in the realities of the present. That meant acknowledging — as Fred often did so memorably — that darkness unbidden is a big part of even the happiest of lives.

One of the more surprising things you learn when you decide to write about life in a small town is how often you feel compelled to write about death. And when the news involved the passing of key and popular people who called this uniquely American small town home, by God, I'd blog about it.

All this is happening as Latrobe gussies up for another turn in the national spotlight. November '19 will see the release of the Fred Rogers movie, "A Beautiful Day in the Neighborhood," with Tom Hanks perfectly cast as Mr. Rogers. As with any national mention, squads of feature writers will visit to profile the vivid, but authentic contrast between Mister Rogers Neighborhood and the real thing.

And to put a cherry on it, I was just handed an unfortunate diagnosis that led many to believe I'm on my way out. I'm fine with that. I don't want to live forever. I want to live right now.

Right here.

Although most of these stories focus on my small town and her surrounding western Pennsylvania communities, ours is a mindset shared by vivacious people in cities large and small from all over the world.

I think it's just an understanding, maybe imbued by our famous neighbor, that we're all destined to die. But living — real living — takes real moxie.

We believe the cliche saying "You only live once!" is pure fraud.

In fact, you only die once.

You're graced with the option to live every single day.

The following stories show how we here in Mister Rogers' Real Neighborhood do it. The stories focus on Fred and his impact on us (and the world), but also the impact the world is having on us. Thus, the book is scattered with life lessons on things like bullying, politics, human nature and what happens when you get tick bit in a sensitive place.

So in the end this book is about living and dying in the personally influential town legends aplenty call home. Fred Rogers especially. It's not a fantasy. It's not a fable. It's not a safe space. It's not make-believe.

It's a real town with real people.

And with this book, I intend to keep it real.

Chris Rodell
June 2019

Foreword

I've been an admirer of Latrobe and her people since way back when I was first invited to visit by the town's No. 1 promoter, our friend, the late Arnold Palmer. I've long marveled at how one seemingly ordinary small town could raise not one, but two, Presidential Medal of Freedom winners, Arnold and Fred Rogers; two men who made global and enduring contributions that are still reverberating and bringing joy and humanity to each new generation.

Was it magic? Was it something in the water? Or maybe something in the Rolling Rock beer, yet another iconic Latrobe native?

I'm closer to finding the elusive answers after reading Chris Rodell's exuberant chronicle of living life in Latrobe. Chris and his family have called Latrobe home since 1992 and the father of two writes about Latrobe the way Sinatra sings about New York, unflinching about the gritty realities, but with abiding affection and relentless positivity about the future.

I became aware of Chris in 2017 when he approached me regarding an interview for a book he was doing about his oddball friendship with Arnold and why a man who could live literally anywhere chose to live in the same small western Pennsylvania steel town where he was born. Arnold lived and died, in fact, in relatively modest homes on the very same street just 320 yards — a well-struck tee shot — from one another.

That book became the award-winning "Arnold Palmer:

Homespun Stories of The King," for my money the most illuminating book anyone has written about Arnold.

Now Latrobe is about to take yet another bow in the national spotlight. Tom Hanks will be starring as Fred Rogers in the Tri-Star pictures release of "A Beautiful Day in the Neighborhood." Moviegoers will wonder, what kind of people could have had a hand in raising a human being so kind, decent, cheerful and loving, so perfectly aspirational?

You're holding the answer in your hands.

As I said in 1999 when, as governor, I was privileged to honor Fred with the Pennsylvania Founder's Award, "He was the man who not only taught us right from wrong, but left from right."

Chris was persuaded that the release of the movie was the perfect time to delve into an archive of more than 2,000 essays and features about living in Mister Rogers' Real Neighborhood — about living in Latrobe. The best of the bunch are in this book.

They are stories of heroism and defeat, struggle and perseverance, tears and laughter — the stories that make up a life well lived.

They are stories of the heart written straight from the heart.

They prove to me Latrobe is lucky to have a writer like Chris Rodell and how lucky America is to have towns like Latrobe.

Honorable Gov. Tom Ridge
June 2019

Author's Note on Profanity ...

The author strives to be faithful to the accuracy, intent and emotion of the situations conveyed on the following pages. Sometimes that requires vivid descriptions, sometimes proper punctuation, sometimes perfect phrasing. And sometimes you have to roll out the big guns. The profane guns. Those really big *!@#-ers.

Ah, profanity, it's everywhere. It's in the newspapers, on the cable news shows and in the hallowed halls of power in our nation's capitol. It sneaks unrehearsed into SNL monologues, in player victory celebration speeches, and is heard from the lecterns of provocative professors.

And, son of a, er, gun, it's even in Mister Rogers' Neighborhood, the real one. In fact, one of the few places you'll be unable to find it is on the pages of this book. It has been decided a book that at heart is about a man who never swore — heck there's scant evidence the man ever even frowned — should not traffic in gutter language. Therefore, any quoted or implied profanity is either paraphrased or sanitized to avoid offending the spirit of Fred. The exceptions being hell, damn, ass, bitch (unavoidable for Chapter 17) and bastard which he gratuitously tossed in near the end because the author was almost done, was beginning to miss typing profanities and didn't really know if anyone was going to read that far anyway.

For those who are disappointed, those who reflexively blurted out "WTF?" the author promises his next book will include profanity.

He swears.

Chapter 1

America's Least Likely Superhero

They were helicopter parents years before most Americans had ever even seen a helicopter. That's what most parenting "experts" would say about the way James and Nancy Rogers raised the baby they named Fred McFeely Rogers, born March 20, 1928. They refused to allow him to mingle with common classmates. They discouraged his tentative strides toward independence. They spoiled him, smothered him with parental love.

What this says about a widely derided parenting technique is best left to the experts, but clearly some children of helicopter parents are destined to soar.

Fred was born into one of the wealthiest families in Westmoreland County. They lived in what was then called a mansion in the affluent part of town known as "The Hill." Nancy Rogers was the daughter of a wealthy industrialist, Fred B. McFeely, founder of McFeely Brick, makers of the heat-resistant bricks that lined the mighty ovens that fueled the thriving steel town's most prominent industry. James Rogers was skilled at business and ran the family interests with prosperous results.

The parents were known, beloved even, for their uncommon generosity and civic-mindedness. They went to painstaking lengths to ensure the needs of struggling Latrobe families were met. An annual Christmas trip to New York City yielded as many as 1,500 gifts to be distributed to Rogers family, friends, employees, and needy recipients around town.

But their prominence and community largesse only served to further isolate the shy, sensitive boy. His privilege left him outside of and suspiciously different from those within the commiserating circles of want.

It didn't help that in 1932, during the depths of the Great Depression, the 20-month-old son of Charles and Anne Morrow Lindbergh was abducted from the international icon's Hopewell, New Jersey, home. Parents around the nation were horrified when the precious toddler's body was found dead, his skull caved in.

Parents became hysterical with fear that if it could happen to Lindbergh, it could happen to them. It could happen in Latrobe. Those who could afford it took extraordinary precautions to ensure the worst didn't happen to them.

That meant Rogers family chauffeur Grant Ross became a critical link in the steadfast family security ring, one that broke just once, but that once was harrowing enough to scar the sensitive boy with an indelible memory that forever shaped his outlook on bullies and a world often short on empathy.

Classes at Latrobe Elementary School were dismissed early one day so Fred began to walk all by himself the 10 blocks home. He told the story during a 1995 speech at Saint Vincent College.

"It wasn't long before I sensed I was being followed — by a whole group of boys. As I walked faster, I looked around. They called my name and came closer and closer and got louder and louder." The wolf pack were yelling, "Freddy! Hey, fat Freddy. We're going to get you, Freddy."

Imagine the terror in that sensitive young boy, the dread of what was going to happen and the inevitability that it would.

He ran as fast as his feet would take him. He made it to a safe house owned by a family friend. She called his mother who swooped in for the rescue.

The very streets where that cruel chase took place would one day be depicted as the model town in the opening scenes of his namesake show that would come to signal comfort and safety to multiple generations of children who were just like him.

The dreadful memory became a tattoo on his fragile, but evolving psyche. It became as much a part of his character as the foundational love of his parents. It fostered a growing need for him to understand the darker aspects of humanity and how to best address them. In the real neighborhood there would be both darkness and light, a vivid contrast that would illuminate the Land of Make-Believe.

The disparity allowed him to become Mister Rogers and as Mister Rogers he could become a real-life crime-fighting superhero as potent as Superman or Captain America. Just ask longtime Latrobe attorney and Rogers family friend Robert Lightcap. Bob and his wife Jo Ann were returning home after attending a Pittsburgh ballet performance when Lightcap's vehicle was set upon by three late teens bent on an urban rampage.

"We were at a red light and they just came up and started beating on the car," he said. "They were rocking the car, pounding on the hood and windows. It was really scary."

What could they do? The terrified occupants didn't have a gun. They didn't need a gun.

They had Mr, Rogers!

"You should have seen it. Fred just rolled down the window and said, 'What do you boys think you're doing?' He was mad, but in complete control. They recognized him right away. One said, 'Hey, it's Mr. Rogers!' Then it was like they instantly reverted to childhood. They just apologized and said they were sorry and were going to go straight home."

The car occupants were still shaken from the encounter as the boys faded down the street. The harassed sat there in silence trying to collect themselves and process what had just happened. The quiet was broken by Fred who commanded, 'Now go!"

One of the most persistent urban legends is that Fred Rogers was either a Navy SEAL, or was an expert Army sniper. Another says he always wore long sleeve sweaters to conceal military kill tattoos.

Nonsense.

That painstaking fact-checkers have been unable to defeat the fables only proves just how much some segments of the public hunger for news that is often too good to be true.

That's what makes the Lightcap story so instructive. It shows that in this often malevolent world it's simply not possible for anyone to grow up to ever be either too good or too true.

It's fair to wonder how the Mister Rogers benevolent persona translates to today's troubled youths, those who must endure active shooter drills and the classmate funerals of opioid ODs. How can Mister Rogers compete with sponsored YouTube influencers?

Let's ask Pat S., 13. Her story is powerful enough to stand up verbatim on its own. She confesses to having been bullied and growing up feeling hopeless and alone.

"I never met Fred Rogers. In fact, he died 3 years before I was born. Yet he is one of the most impactful people in my life.

"I was having a rough time with basically everything until I saw the 'Won't You Be My Neighbor?' documentary. I've been exposed to Mr. Rogers all my life since I'm from Pittsburgh, but this film really changed my perspective of him. Magically, he was more than the puppet man. He was in a way, my savior. After the film I threw myself into researching him and almost everyone involved with the show. I finally, willingly, got the help I needed.

"I've had my ups and downs but I'll always have Fred's encouragement no matter where I go. I've also met countless people from the show including Joanne Rogers! I hope to go into children's television or the museum field in order to honor Fred one day. Thank you for everything, I'm eternally grateful! 143!"

Fred Rogers: Gone 16 years. Still a life-saving superhero.

A 2008 survey of 3,000 British teenagers found that no fewer than 20 percent of them thought Winston Churchill to be a fictional character. The same survey found that 58 percent thought Sherlock Holmes and 47 percent thought Eleanor Rigby were real people.

Imagine today the write-in votes Harry Potter would score.

Maybe our neighbor's legacy is destined to lead the real Mister Rogers straight back to the Land of Make-Believe. It usually happens when some men and women seem too good to be true.

Chapter 2

Gandhi, MLK ... & Fred Rogers?

America used to really watch Fred Rogers. His show debuted October 15, 1962, and aired 886 episodes — 414 hours — before concluding August 31, 2001. The generation-spanning series could be seen in reruns on PBS another six years.

In March 2018, on-line video streaming platform Twitch.TV in cooperation with the Fred Rogers Company livestreamed the show's entire 31-year run without interruption. Viewers were encouraged to donate to their local PBS station throughout the marathon. The livestream was viewed more than 7.4 million times.

Typical viewer reaction was like that of Kristin W., of Pittsburgh. She told reporters she started watching the marathon at 7 a.m. on Wednesday and kept the program running in the background as she worked. "Listening to Mister Rogers and his message of love and acceptance is a great reminder that not everything in the world is upsetting, frustrating, or otherwise disappointing. Just the opposite, in fact. You can always find a silver lining and a reason to love."

So, yes, it seems America will always watch Mister Rogers.

Given the fact, maybe now it's time America began to really study him.

What could he teach us? How would society benefit from his example? Would civility across America improve if Mister Rogers 101 became part of our school curriculum?

If that happens, it'll happen thanks in part to two Ohio educators — one a now-retired native Latrobean, the other something of a Fred Rogers apostle. They're Bob Rusbosin and Tyler Bradshaw, two men spearheading a nascent movement to persuade the world to view Fred Rogers, not as a popular children's TV host, but instead as a transcendent cultural figure along the lines of Mohandas Gandhi and Martin Luther King Jr.

"I think," Rusbosin says, "we've reached a point where people are yearning for an authentic human being capable of being a role model for civility and all that's good. That's what Fred's been all along."

Rusbosin, today retired and living in Venice, Florida, is nurturing the efforts of Bradshaw to persuade fellow educators of the merits of teaching the full story of Fred. Bradshaw needs little extracurricular motivation. He is an associate director of admissions at Miami University in Oxford, Ohio. He says we severely under-value Fred and all he's done when we think of him merely as a TV puppeteer.

"He's too much of an important figure for history to ignore," Bradshaw says. "I still find myself in complete awe of the man and the movement he created. Other educators are very receptive any time I bring up Fred's name. Once Fred becomes the topic of conversation, however, there's always a warm smile, a tender glow, and a welcome desire to talk about a favorite episode or quote. It's wonderful to have a research subject and personal hero in Fred whom you know nearly everyone will have a positive reaction."

Think of the reaction of any conference attendee used to immersing his or herself in talks about, say, attendance, knowledge retention or staving off professional burn-out and hearing your topic would instead be, ahhh, the life and lessons of Mr. Rogers.

"Those who attended our first conference presentation were overjoyed by the model and the topics we discussed."

And when properly presented, it is truly instructive.

Rogers, Bradshaw says, exhibited four core behaviors that all emotionally developed adults should strive to exude. Doing so will help each of us create what the pair calls an emotional intelligence necessary to be well-rounded and open-minded individuals. These are:

- Authenticity: Fred was wholly comfortable being who he was. He didn't waste any emotional or physical energy pretending he was something he wasn't. "In every moment and every area of his life, Fred was consistent, reliable, and never duplicitous," Bradshaw says.
- Vulnerability: Being vulnerable leads to compassion and builds intimacy. How often in his show did Fred allow himself to be cheerfully humbled before a 6-year-old know-it-all? "Unlike most males of his generation, Fred shared his innermost feelings and opened up to an audience of millions on a daily basis--how rarely are we willing to open up to even our small circle of family and friends in the way Fred did with a nationwide audience?"
- Civility: Try and picture Mr. Rogers in a road rage incident or smirking after posting something nasty on Facebook. It's not easy, is it? Now try and recall how you must have looked last time you succumbed to those primal emotions and if any good came from it. Bradshaw says, "Fred didn't always agree with everyone, but he was always civil and behaved honorably."
- Curiosity: Bradshaw fondly remembers episodes like the ones where Mr. Rogers went to the crayon factory. A curious mind is essential to fresh learning, expanded empathy, and the serendipitous discoveries about people, places, and things that lead to happier humans. "Curiosity acts as the fuel that continues to drive our desire to be authentic, vulnerable, and civil," he says.

"The combination adds up to Fred Rogers and his essential message," Bradshaw says. "I think people who are critical get frustrated with Fred because he succeeded with a message that was so simple and uncluttered. But that's exactly who he was. And there will always be an element of people who believe you can't be a real leader if you're soft-spoken and preach kindness. "Fred proved those people wrong," he says, "and his legacy continues to do that each and every day."

The educators were able to apply their theories to Miami U.'s Hamilton campus when Rusbosin was a senior associate dean of students and Bradshaw was on student government. Some female students were seen viciously mocking a disabled student in a public space. The outrage and the timing, coupled as it was with a national debate over the loss of civility, sparked a drive by the student government to resist the rise of rudeness on campus.

If you think college students wouldn't give a (hoot), you're right.

They instead gave wooden nickels. Thousands of them.

"We developed a campaign that had students giving one another wooden nickels each time they observed one another doing something uncommonly kind," said Rusbosin. "We called it Project Civility."

The project Poster Boy? Fred Rogers.

"The polarization of society has everyone searching for a unifying figure with a message of love and authenticity," Rusbosin says. "And that's Fred."

Students from all walks of life suddenly began making eye contact with and smiling at strangers they used to ignore. Once rapid-fire drive-by conversations slowed to a stroll and became more thoughtful.

And one or two cardigan sweaters made an on-campus appearance.

"I was astounded at how people responded to Project Civility's simplicity — it was the same way people responded to Fred's show," says Bradshaw, who was at the time still a student, albeit one of the project's most enthusiastic participants.

"Project Civility was nothing more than saying a kind word to someone, and handing them a wooden nickel. But how many times might that kind word have been just the hope that someone needed to persevere through a difficult day? And how many times did that wooden nickel become a tangible reminder to someone that they were loved, that they mattered, and that they were special just by being you"? It was a project that Fred would have designed, and it was evidence that his pedagogy is just as powerful with young children as it is with adults--and maybe even more powerful because, as adults, we tend to lose sight of some of those most basic, loving instincts that made our childhoods so wonderful. Fred reminded all of us of that daily."

Eventually — and perhaps inevitably — the pair made a pilgrimage to Latrobe where Rusbosin, the Latrobe native, experienced an awakening.

"Growing up in Latrobe, I was more impressed," he says, "by the sight of Arnold Palmer landing his private jet after some distant victory. The guy with the puppets was kind of hokey to me. I was suspicious of him, too. I doubted anyone could be that genuine."

Then he began to see his old neighbor through new, youthful eyes. "Tyler would quote Fred with such sincerity," he said. "I became intrigued. I'm now convinced had Fred Rogers focused on college students the way he did on children today he'd be a legend among educators and student development professionals."

He believes that's exactly where Bradshaw's work will lead. After meeting the people and seeing the sites, it all came together for Bradshaw. He could tell Latrobe was the perfect incubator for the boy who would become the man.

"You can just see the way a town like Latrobe would influence someone like Fred, he said. "That's the kind of community where you go to raise good kids."

Bradshaw says he was struck by an almost hyper-curiosity of the townsfolk. Every introduction led to a cheerful interrogation. "They wanted to know if I had a girlfriend, where I was from — everything."

The native curiosity is, as noted, a hallmark of happy people. So impressed was he by the character of the people that he made a focus of recruiting Latrobe-area students to attend Miami.

The people from Mister Rogers' Neighborhood are intuitively aware of the lessons of Fred Rogers, he says, "and, for me, every important lesson I've learned in life I've learned in Mister Rogers's Neighborhood."

Sadly, some of those lessons can break your heart. Bradshaw was forced to learn one of them July 24, 2013, when he became a survivor of suicide. His father, as buoyant and loving a father a son could ever hope to have, surrendered to his depression.

In www.SeeYaBub.com, his poignant and powerful blog about the death and its earthly repercussions, Bradshaw explores how we deal with grief that seems insurmountable and how we learn to persevere.

"The blog is a labor of love," he says, "but I told myself that if I get to the other side and my Creator tells me that there was one person who contemplated suicide but chose another route because of my writing/speaking through the blog, it will have been worth all the effort I put in. Fred taught me to slow down in the aftermath of losing my Dad. He taught me to appreciate the simple wonder of a conversation with a loved one. He taught me the value of listening to my own thoughts and feelings and putting those things into words to help my grief. He taught me what it meant to be a grieving man who believed in a hopeful tomorrow."

The key, they say, is to raise awareness of the soulful benefits of teaching students about the life and philosophies of Fred Rogers and then watching the kindling catch fire.

Think about it. Our children learn extensive lessons about our generals who secure important victories.

Who knows? Maybe if students learn the lessons of the man skilled at the art of kindness we'll one day reduce the need for those skilled at the art of war.

Chapter 3

Is Latrobe Truly Special?

Our small town self-deprecations are so pronounced that when Smithsonian Magazine in '17 declared Latrobe one of America's best small towns, many of the people who live here by choice said, "Who? Us?" It's like being voted Miss America and demanding a recount.

The Smithsonian's overview description didn't seem to apply to fair Latrobe, which seemed, well, fair enough:

"There's something about small towns that ignite our imaginations. Maybe it's the charming main streets lined with century-old structures, now filled with artisan shops and cozy family-owned breakfast eateries, or the meandering rivers that run through downtown centers and majestic mountains that rise in the not-too-far distance, offering access to a world of activity. Or perhaps it's one-of-a-kind museums, attractions and festivities that are brimming with hometown pride."

I could only imagine the throbbing consternation in promotional boardrooms of tonier nearby burghs like Ligonier and Bedford, two small towns noted for charming main streets lined with century-old structures, now filled with artisan shops and cozy family-owned breakfast eateries, or the meandering rivers that run through downtown centers and majestic mountains that rise in the not-too-far distance, offering access to a world of activity.

So to speak.

Is Latrobe special and if so, what makes it special?

It certainly wasn't special in 1998, at least not in the eyes of Esquire magazine writer Tom Junod. It was Junod, you may recall, who wrote the article about Fred Rogers that inspired the ballyhood Tom Hanks movie. I read the article when it appeared under the headline: "Can You Say ... Hero?" The subhead reads, "Fred Rogers has been doing the same small good things for a very long time."

It's a tremendous piece of writing. Descriptive and movingly poignant, it should be handed out to every movie goer as they depart the film. That article helped Mr. Rogers transcend a sort of cult figure to mainstream appreciation. What was once proper — acknowledging the cultural of Fred Rogers — had suddenly become cool.

And for years the only precise words I could recall from the entire piece were the slam on the town I was proud to call home.

"… sad, fading Latrobe."

"And so we went to the graveyard. We were heading there all along, because Mister Rogers *loves* graveyards, and so as we took the long, straight road out of sad, fading Latrobe, you could still feel the *speed* in him, the hurry, as he mustered up a sad anticipation, and when we passed through the cemetery gates, he smiled as he said to Bill Isler, "The plot's at the end of the yellow-brick road."

Sad? Fading?

Today, I think he'd describe it as gleeful and ascending.

I asked some neighbors if they thought Latrobe was special. Spoiler alert ... they do! Their responses are interesting in that none of them cited the charming main streets lined with century-old structures, now filled with artisan shops and cozy family-owned breakfast eateries ...

The first person I spoke with has an informed and rosy outlook, which is helpful because her name is Rosie, too. She's Latrobe Mayor Rosie Wolford and, yes, I think it makes us special that we're led by an optimist named Rosie. "Oh, yes, Latrobe is special," Wolford says. "And much of that is due to the spirit of Fred Rogers. He's still such a big part of our lives. His voice still matters."

She cites the tangible impact of The McFeely-Rogers Foundation and its focus on community and recreation. Fred's driving vision is the reason Latrobe is celebrated for its park programs, its exercise paths and competitive opportunities that aim to keep youth fit and off the phones.

In Latrobe, the trolley is to town identity what little green men are to Roswell, New Mexico. The trolley tops our street signs; there's a trolley replica for children to play on in the Legion-Keener playland. It's stationary, but in the minds of generations of children that charming playground fixture has traveled farther than any Roswell alien. And there's a bumper sticker on the Tin Lizzy fridge they use to frost the beer mugs that declares, "My Other Car Is A Trolley."

Family day draws Rogers fans to Latrobe each June and Wolford says eyes light up when she's at out-of-town conferences and people hear she's mayor of someplace special.

"The Mr. Rogers link is a huge plus for Latrobe," she says. "I was just at a conference in Lancaster. We gave fellow attendees Mr. Rogers cups. They were a huge hit. It's always a reminder of how much our neighbor meant to the world, and how we all need carry on Fred's vision for kindness. Happily, he's entwined in everything we do here in Latrobe."

Tom Kennedy is senior pastor at Latrobe's United Methodist Church. He says the spirit of Mr. Rogers leads to a euphoric kind of volunteerism like he's never experienced any place else. "Oh, there's far more volunteerism and community involvement than any place I've served. I wouldn't even say it's second nature. In Latrobe, helping people is reflexive. I don't know if it started with Fred Rogers, but it's his message that today still inspires so many."

The message is often reinforced from the pulpit. Kennedy says often when he's giving a sermon about community involvement he'll circle back to Fred.

"Here in Latrobe, he's still such a big part of our daily lives. Reminders of him are in our storefronts, on our signposts, on our bridges and now we can see his statue almost every day."

He says in Latrobe it's not unusual to find people with many life obligations to carve out time in their busy day to stop and chat with residents at the senior center; one gentleman in particular makes a point of doing so. "It's in this town where I've experienced more humble acts like that than anywhere else," Kennedy says. "It's everywhere, sure, but there's just more of it here, more looking out for the least, the lost, or the ones out on the fringe. And I have to believe much of that is due to Fred and his on-going influence."

Steve Limani lives in a home right across the street from Fred Rogers' boyhood home. A Pennsylvania State Trooper, he has an unusual gauge as to why we're special:

Even our bad guys have good manners.

It's been that way from Day 1 after he'd transferred in from eastern Pennsylvania, a part of the Keystone State so infamous for coarse behavior it might as well be New Jersey.

"Every time I'd pull someone over out there it was the same thing every day for five straight years — just a verbal thrashing," he says. "It was always, 'Don't you have anything better to do?' Or they'd have physically uncomfortable suggestions on what I could do with the ticket. It was all day, every day. Just constant hostility. It really got to you."

So he was wearing psychological body armor when he pulled over his first speeding motorist near Latrobe. But the culprit didn't rebel. He didn't (complain). He didn't offer any proctological disposal suggestions. He offered instead something that caught Limani by surprise. He confessed.

"First thing the guy did was say he was sorry. He said, "Yes, trooper. I was speeding. No excuses." I just walked back and wrote up the ticket and handed it to him. That's when he surprised me again. He said, 'Thank you.'"

The proverbial welcome wagon would triumph over the figurative paddy wagon. "It was July and smokin' hot. The guy says, 'Here, trooper,' and hands me an iced bottle of water. 'I had extra and you look like you could use it.' He was right. I was dripping sweat, but I was dumbfounded by the gesture. He put it in my hand and slowly pulled away."

How calloused had Limani become by hostility? He suspected the gift water might be … poison!

"I went back to the cruiser and inspected it carefully. It wasn't opened and I was thirsty. But I was too skeptical of kindness to drink it."

Back at the barracks, his colleagues explained a homespun mindset he's since come to live by: "There are a lot of good people in this world. And a good many of them live right around here."

Latrobe, of course, is no utopia where our police spend their days handing out to lollipops and balloon animals to fresh-faced school children. Murder, armed robbery, drug-related crime — they all happen here in roughly the same percentages as they do in comparable towns.

But Latrobe police Sgt. Joe Angus says while the bad people may be bad, the good people are very good.

"Latrobe is a great town to be a police officer," he says. "There are just so many truly kind people here. The community support and the support from our mayor and council are very strong."

Both the Latrobe and McFeely-Rogers foundations are generous with their contributions whenever need arises, and he cites consistent generosity from private citizens, in particular Robindale Energy president Scott Kroh and his family, for their support.

The goodwill gestures extend clear down to the dinner table. Angus says it's not uncommon for fellow diners to pick up the check anytime they see uniformed officers out for a bite.

As the barracks spokesman, Limani is entrusted with a highly visible role in the community. He's the one who appears on all the TV newscasts when newsworthy crime is committed. In addition, he's the trooper invited into our churches, schools and meeting halls to explain and promote citizen involvement. He knows the community and its people — good and bad — as well as anyone.

"I swear, Latrobe is beyond special," he says. "The people are kind and the community tight-knit. It's a place I'm excited and proud to call home. For a tiny town, we have some of the most impactful people who have walked the face of this earth."

It's changed him, he says. He thinks back to his first encounter with the friendly speeder and how differently he'd have handled it today.

"That younger guy was too suspicious to even accept an ice-cold water on a blistering hot day. The current version woulda been (socializing) with the guy on the side of the road over a cold one. We'd have become friends."

Living in Latrobe makes following some cardinal parenting rules difficult for naturally friendly folk like Briana Tomack. As a parent of two boys, she's admonished them on the inherent risks of talking to strangers. Then she'd confuse the boys by smiling sunshine at each potential threat. She'd say hello, asks how they were doing. By God, she'd treat each of these potential threats like they were, yikes, potential friends.

"I'd spend all this time telling my kids not to talk to strangers then I'd have to explain to them at the park why I spent so much time laughing and talking to strangers."

In Latrobe no one's a stranger for long. As president of the Greater Latrobe-Laurel Valley Chamber of Commerce, she's now paid to do what she's for years done for free: gush about living in Latrobe. Like others she talks often about Fred Rogers and his enduring influence.

"In Latrobe, Fred Rogers is stitched into the fabric of everything we do," she says. "The kindness, cheer and understanding he is known for to this day is something that warms our identity."

Tomack is quick to point out the more tangible reasons that make Latrobe special, foremost being Steeler training camp at Saint Vincent, a celebration of one of the NFL's most historic franchises on fields named in honor of revered four-time Super Bowl champion coach Chuck Noll (unavoidable joke interjection: "Dallas can keep its grassy knoll; Saint Vincent is proud to have Noll-ey grass.")

Steeler training camp, now in its 54th year, draws as many as 10,000 fans each day from all over the country. They fill the hotels, drink at our bars, eat at our restaurants and make each late summer both hectic and happy.

"It's just another reason why we love living here," she says. "It's a place where people will always feel really connected to our roots. The friends we grew up with are today some of the same ones teaching our children. We also have all these great parks and recreational opportunities. Those of us who live here truly love it. It is special."

Attorney Bob Lightcap has lived here all his life, long enough to recall a Latrobe of days gone by that was what he considers more special than it is today. The reason? A host of locally-owned businesses.

"Back when Fred and I were growing up in Latrobe all the prominent employers were locally owned," he says. "So everyone — from the custodian to the CEO — had a stake in Latrobe succeeding. All the people running the businesses had kids in the Latrobe schools. They all played on the same teams. Local ownership makes a difference and that's something we've lost and will likely never get back."

He makes a good point, but that's happening around the country.

Others will contend Latrobe is special because even if we didn't have Fred Rogers to inspire us we'd have women like Ronda Buchman Goetz, third-generation owner of Rose's Style Shoppe a Latrobe institution since 1932. "My grandmother all those years ago started out determined to create a place that was more than your typical business," Goetz says.

"She sold dresses and accessories, but what made her store special was that she created a place of joy, a safe haven. A place where everyone feels comfortable and at home. It's what we're still doing today.

"In towns like Latrobe, we all learn by example of others" she says. "And we are fortunate to have the message and example of Mister Rogers. He has taught us about unconditional love, kindness, and the ability to find the good in others. That's what makes Latrobe so special."

So is Latrobe truly special? Who's to say? But on most days just truly believing you're special can make a real difference.

Fred Rogers thought Latrobe was special. He conceived a legend based in part in that heartfelt conviction.

He felt that same special conviction about folks like you and me, too.

Life Lesson on ...

Our Neighborhood Opioid crisis

It was 4:45 p.m. October 19, 2017. I was home and Val could sense I was beginning to feel anxious. I had somewhere I had to be. Was I late for Happy Hour? No. I was late for prayer. In some ways I was late for an Unhappy Hour.

I'd accepted an invitation to attend a prayer service in recognition of the opioid abuse crisis that's poisoning all America. It's happening in big cities and small. And it's happening right here in Mister Rogers' Neighborhood.

The Greater Latrobe Ministerial Association chose to host the service under the bright autumnal sunshine in the Fred Rogers Memorial Park under the smiling gaze of Fred's statue. It was appropriate for reasons I suspect I alone knew.

See, I know a secret about Fred Rogers, one I've been reluctant to share since 1993 when I was paid to share it with, oh, about 6 million strangers.

Fred Rogers did time in rehab.

That was the story I wrote for *National Enquirer*. It was back when I was in the midst of glorious 10-year run of wacky stories for what was then America's most notorious newspaper.

I remember in vivid detail how I secured the facts. I'd been sipping beers with my buddy Paul and Jimmy Plazza, the late owner of The Lantern, a popular Latrobe tavern that once sat on the spot that's now the senior living facility where my dear mother spent her last year.

The bar phone rang. It was Val calling to say my *Enquirer* editor called with an assignment about Saint Fred. I was instantly dismayed. I correctly surmised it would be something unflattering which my revealing would make me a pariah among certain elements of Latrobe society. As you're about to learn, none of those elements were right then drinking hootch in The Lantern.

I told Paul. Sitting and overhearing about four stools down was the late Dickie Kemp. He died relatively young — he was 64 — in 2017 of natural causes after many years of indulging abundant vices. We all liked Dickie very much.

He heard the name Fred Rogers and piped right up: "Fred Rogers? I was just in rehab with his son. I met Fred when he'd come to visit. Great guy. What's the story about?"

I pulled a fifty out of my wallet and told Dickie to slide on down. I'd be buying all night. Just like that, I had my "A" source. I just sat and listened to him tell me his story of how he was kicking one addiction while I, now all of a sudden on the expense account, was abetting another.

The thrust of the story was how the scourge of drugs can happen to even the most loving of families. But the best part was how Fred, an ordained Presbyterian minister, set up an impromptu ministry right there in the rehab rec yard.

"When we saw him, everyone started cracking up and mocking him. Some of it was pretty vicious. A lot of these guys were hard-core junkies," Dickie said. "But one-by-one, every one of these lowlifes went up to him and started telling him their stories. And one by one, they all started bawling. He just had so much compassion. He was saving lives."

In the years to come, I'd interview Arnold Palmer more than 100 times, but Dickie's revelation led to the only in-person encounter I'd ever have with our famous neighbor. The full story on this is told later in this book.

Does anyone remember seeing a "60 Minutes" expose on the origins of the opioid crisis? I can't remember being more appalled by a news report.

Most of the news that appalls is instigated by men and women Dickie would call lowlifes. What happened with Congress, the DEA and the drug distributor overlords was conducted by scores of people with respectable pedigrees. They're educated, attend church, serve on boards of prestigious charitable organizations.

And they all sold their souls to medicate ours.

Are we all doomed to live in an age when the lowlifes are the leaders?

My pastor told me she was recently summoned to the hospital to inform three young children their 29-year-old mother had died. The kids will be raised by their grandparents. Their father ODd years ago.

An attending friend told me he knew of the deaths of six classmates in the last few months. He's 38.

Every single day the local obituaries feature another smiling face of someone too young to die.

This is Latrobe, Mister Rogers' Neighborhood, the town we've chosen to raise our children.

So what do I hope to accomplish by telling this story? I don't know, but I hope prayers help.

Because I fear we're approaching a day when the dead outnumber those who still care.

Chapter 4

Relevant Landmarks

First of all, you have to leave Latrobe and drive 3 miles if you want to get to either the Latrobe airport, the Latrobe high school or Latrobe Country Club. To add to the confusion, the town where those three landmark properties are (sorta) located shares the name with an Ohio steel town that pops up on GPS map apps and directs motorists 106 miles out of the way when all the further they need to go is, oh, 1 mile.

"Yeah, being the Youngstown Grille in Youngstown, Pennsylvania, has led to its share of confusion," says restaurant owner Scott Levin. If it ever happens to you and you wind up in the Buckeye State, it's worth persisting through the hunger to return to (sorta) Latrobe for your meal. Readers of the local papers have voted Scott's place as the best breakfast in town.

Interestingly, there are no roads named after either Arnold Palmer or Fred Rogers in Latrobe proper. They're both in Youngstown. Fred grew up on Weldon Street in Latrobe and eventually took ownership of Tudor Manor, a summer family retreat at the eastern end of Youngstown's Main Street, now named Fred Rogers Drive.

The western end of that same street is today named Arnold Palmer Drive. Palmer was born in a house on that street in 1929 and was residing in a house just up the same street in 2016 when he died. A man who could have been pampered in palaces around the planet never really left Latrobe, er, Youngstown.

It's why I in 2018 argued we should change the name from Youngstown to Palmerville. As movements go, this one was mostly stationary and confined to my afternoon bar stool at The Tin Lizzy. Still I'm convinced the idea should be adopted because of its ample merits.

This sounds facetious, but I'm serious. How serious?

I've pestered former Pennsylvania Gov. and Homeland Security Secretary Tom Ridge to get involved. Arnold Palmer has no greater booster than Ridge. Here's some of what Ridge said told me for my 2018 "Palmer: Homespun" book that leads me to believe he's at heart supportive:

"There's no question there's an enormous appetite to perpetuate his legacy," Ridge says. "People are always going to want to see the town where Arnold Palmer grew up, see his workshop, his office, his memorabilia and play the course where he grew up."

Arnold Palmer put Youngstown on the map. It's time we return the favor.

But if you're ever in town for one reason or another, here's a jiffy local's guide about Fred-related things to do:

Childhood home of Fred Rogers
737 Weldon Street

You may wind up getting your mug shot taken by The Man if you're lingering too long outside the childhood home of Fred Rogers. The "Man" is not there to hassle you. He's just being neighborly. "It happens all the time," says Tpr. Steve Limani, who lives just across the street from the landmark home. "People come from all over to admire the house where Mr, Rogers was raised and ask if I wouldn't mind taking their picture. I'm happy to do it." The home is now occupied by one of our civic leaders devoted to making Latrobe even more livable. Limani says the home is becoming a bona fide tourist attraction. "I had no idea how big a deal Mr, Rogers was until I moved in right across the street from his childhood home. You wouldn't believe the impressive number of tourists from all over who want to see Mr, Rogers's Real Neighborhood. And they all want a picture."

Fred Rogers Statue
James Hillis Rogers Park
Jefferson & Main Streets.

As many know, Fred was enamored with weighing precisely 143 pounds throughout his life because of its soulful numeric symbolism — "I Love You!" Who knows what he'd make out of ballooning up to 300 pounds in posterity. That's how much the Jon Hair bronze sculpture dedicated in 2016 weighs. In just three years, the statue has become a tourist attraction and a focal point for civic events like Mister Rogers Family Days every June. Mayor Rosie Wolford says. "The Fred statue is an important addition to our downtown. Fred has contributed so much to his hometown, not just while he was alive but continuously, each and every day. We Latrobeans celebrate Fred every day as we live the life he envisioned, that of being a good neighbor and sharing the love that is Latrobe." History bolsters her enthusiasm. The statue has the dynamic potential of being an inert Latrobe revitalization program. It'd be a mistake to dismiss the impact pop culture statues like this one can have on a town's future. A critically panned statue of "Happy Days" character Arthur Fonzarelli along Milwaukee's Riverwalk is estimated to have earned the city the equivalent of $14 million in free PR. And purely in terms of cultural impact, The Forged Fred could kick the butt of The Bronze Fonz.

Latrobe Art Center
819 Ligonier Street

I've long argued that the nearer your tattoo joint to the center of town than your most prominent cultural concern, the more likely your town fountain is apt to smell funny. Screwball theories aside, it's becoming clear the 2002 opening of the Latrobe Art Center was a big boost to downtown Latrobe. Founded by the late Nancy Rogers Crozier (Fred's sister) and Elizabeth Hazlett, the center has fostered a vibrant artistic community in the heart of Latrobe intent on making Latrobe more beautiful and more livable. The center — it's a cafe, too! — offers art classes, programs, workshops, as well as hosting community events and gatherings. The center is located on the same block as was Tassell Pharmacy, where druggist David Strickler invented the first banana split.

McFeely-Rogers Memorial Pool
Legion-Keener Park

There's no record of Fred Rogers ever swimming in the refreshing park pool paid for and still supported by the family of Fred Rogers. But every Latrobe child who's ever taken a dip in the scenic park pool owes some gratitude to the McFeely-Rogers and Latrobe foundations. The pool is a sparkling keystone of a 52-acre recreational mecca that includes multiple playgrounds, athletic fields, a concert band shell, and scenic creekside walkways along the banks of the rambling Loyalhanna Creek. The Playland pays tribute to Mister Rogers' Neighborhood with a magical trolley toddlers with any imagination can steer clear to the moon.

Adams Memorial Library
1112 Ligonier St.

The local library, funded by monies earned by Fred Rogers and Arnold Palmer, had from 2000-2018 the only branch library that required daily runway clearance before it helped our imaginations take off. The Adams Memorial Library had "Mo," its popular bookmobile stationed in an airport hangar each night after it made its daily rounds. But after an 18-year run of 132,169 miles — that's a lot of miles for a vehicle that rarely strayed beyond the borders — it was decommissioned and sold to a Kentucky business man looking for a mobile office. A pity. Chief librarian Tracey Trotter remembers the exuberance of Fred Rogers the day Mo took to the road. It was July 4, 2000, a Yankee Doodle Dandy birthday for a bookmobile. "I remember Fred was so happy about taking all these books to so many children and their parents," she said. There is talk, she said, of obtaining another one, but the internet — that soulless destructor of all that was once considered quaint and charming — has reduced the need. I'm happy our daughters' childhoods include memories of waiting for Mo to roll up, and for all the indelible curiosity-sparking moments-that hometown library has bestowed. It's because of Adams Memorial Library I advise people if they want to appear more colorful to get a tattoo. If they want to become more colorful get a library card.

Fred Rogers Center
Saint Vincent College

The $14-million, 36,000-square-foot, state-of-the-art hall is like its namesake in that it's monumental. Opened in 2008, the center is dedicated to preserving the lofty standards for teaching and nurturing children set by Fred. It has 16,000 documents outlining his thinking, interactive exhibits as well as some nifty Rogers show memorabilia on permanent display. So it's been a boon for researchers and students intent on extending his work, but it's also become special to Latrobe for hosting events that welcome the public. During a poignant mingling of two Latrobe legends, the Center was host to the joyful reception following the 2016 passing of Arnold Palmer. It's magnificent and thus one of the places that most exalts Fred Rogers at the same time refutes one of his bedrock convictions. Fred said: "I've often hesitated in the beginning a project because I've thought, 'It'll never turn out to be even remotely like the good idea I have as

I start." Applied to the center, it proves him wrong. The Fred Rogers Center is better than anyone imagined it could be.

Greater Latrobe Senior High School
131 High School Rd.

It, to me, is the best kind of subversive education because high school students walk past the Fred Rogers display and probably never realize it's whispering to them. It's saying, "Psst … Be Kind … Be Inclusive … Love thy Neighbor." It's like in the Latrobe high school, Fred Rogers gets away with saying things Jesus never could. The display is only open to the public during scheduled school activities. But kids see it every day. They unwittingly absorb the message that being good is good.

Final Resting Place
Unity Cemetery
114 Chapel Lane

Fred Rogers is interred in a Rogers family mausoleum with his loved ones. It overlooks beautiful views of the Chestnut Ridge branch of the Laurel Highlands, views that for century beguile people into never leaving. Fred spent most of his adult life residing in Pittsburgh, but in the end he came home to Latrobe for good. His remains are interred in his ancestral Given family mausoleum.

DeNunzio's Restaurant at Arnold Palmer Regional Airport

In Latrobe, we go for satisfying meals and camaraderie to two transportation depots where people in other towns go to get the hell out of town. Sure we do that, too, at the train station and the Arnold Palmer Regional Airport, but we always (most of us) include in our purchase return tickets. Planes have been using the one-time pasture since 1924 and it first became famous in 1939 when it became the site of the world's first official airmail pickup. The planes so nearby and visible made a profound impact on a young man who reflexively broke one of golf's cardinal rules anytime a plane flew overhead. Arnold Palmer couldn't help it. He'd lift his head. He became such an enthusiastic aviator and booster of the local airport (he served for years on the airport authority) they named the whole facility after him in 1999. A statue of him leaning on a golf club graces the green space between the parking lot and the front entrance. The thriving airport — free parking! — is home to Spirit airlines and the wildly popular Westmoreland County Airshow, often featuring headliner acts like the Blue Angels, the Thunderbirds or the Canadian Forces Snowbirds. Thus, it's a tribute to the chef that what goes on up in the air is only slightly more thrilling than what goes on the plate. Since 2004, DeNunzio's is not only a hometown favorite, but a favorite for international travelers in town to do business at Kennametal, Westmoreland Mechanical Testing & Research, Aggressive Grinding or any of the other international businesses that call Latrobe home. So for some engineer from, say, Mumbai, India, DeNunzio's might be a special treat in an out-of-the-way locale. For Latrobe, we're happy it's right where it is.

DiSalvo's Station
325 McKinley Ave.

I mean this as no slight to Joe DiSalvo or his fine restaurant, but some of my best times I've had at his restaurant have happened sitting outside his restaurant eating take-out sandwiches. Yes in Latrobe it's acceptable to take Subways to the train station. We do it five or six times a summer when the forecast looks pleasant and someone suggests "train lunch?" Then we'll stop and get some hoagies and a pocketful of pennies and head to the old train station. The doomed pennies are placed on the track for artistic squashing. It's good, cheap conversation-nurturing fun. There's just something so exciting about being 10 feet from a 200-ton locomotive as it pulls 100 cars east bound for New York City, a city full of devoted foodies who if they knew what they were doing would board that train and take it straight back to DiSalvo's for a memorable feast in an unforgettable setting. Whenever I want to impress high-class friends visiting Latrobe, I take them to the main floor at DiSalvo's. Where do I take anyone I want to impress? Downstairs at DiSalvo's. The lower floor is a plush cigar bar and is one of the coolest places in town. I've been going there 25 years and anytime anyone suggests, hey, let's go to DiSalvo's, I've never once said, ah, do we have to? I'll go every time. Again and again and again. It's a happy habit.

The Tin Lizzy
Main St., Youngstown

Your first thought when stepping through the varnished doors at the historic Tin Lizzy will probably be, "Man, this place must be really, really old." The last thought when you depart many happy hours later will likely be, "Man, this place is really, really cool!" And you'll be right both times. Experts have determined the building's foundational elements date to clear back to the '50s. The 1750's, that is. The vestiges of that epoch are evident in the buildings timbering, its fireplaces and a lively aura known to attract everyone from ghostbusters to connoisseurs of charm and ambiance. And the only thing more enchanting than the Tin Lizzy's past is its glorious present. It's the best place to visit if you're seeking conviviality and good food. Of course, I'm biased. My office since 2015 has been on the top floor of the 3-story Tin. There's a basement Rathskeller, a street-level bar favored by locals, and a beguiling martini bar and deck on the 2nd floor. Arnold Palmer's father used to live here when it was a hotel and Palmer himself was a frequent guest. It's my social and occupational base. I've had people ask me what I do when I'm not having fun at The Tin Lizzy. I tell them it hasn't happened yet, but if it ever does I'll just go someplace else in The Tin Lizzy.

Life Lesson on ...

Crowded Funerals

I may be posting "Help Wanted" ads in the next few weeks. I'm thinking of hiring about 200 part-time actors who I'll pay to attend the funerals of deceased clients intent on memorable send-offs.

This brainstorm occurred to me in October 2016 as I was sitting there in the pew mourning Arnold Palmer. I've been to weddings that were less uplifting. A veritable who's who of golf and business celebrities brought tears to our eyes as we eulogized this great man for his philanthropy, his warmth and his sporting achievements. The Golf Channel covered the whole thing live, including the ceremonial jet fly-over at the conclusion.

It's a petty admission, I know, but I became envious.

I realized my funeral would be nothing like his.

Instead of a line of private jets circling over the airport named in my honor, there'd be ample parking with just a few duct-taped jalopies outside Latrobe's cheapest local funeral home.

It saddens me, sure, but I prefer being sad to being busy piling up the time-consuming accomplishments it'd take to ensure a well-attended funeral.

I thought if only I could pay people to show up and say nice things about me it might lessen the sting my survivors feel at being stiffed in the will. Sure, it'd be better if they were actual friends telling the truth, but any lying stranger will do in a pinch.

I believe many people will agree — and pay for the privilege.

How much would you pay to ensure 100 soulful weepers showed up at your funeral? Maybe $1,000? Maybe $2,500? Of course, warm bodies to mourn a cold one is just the beginning.

I envision tiered levels of escalating services.

I contend having a sultry blonde stranger attending the funeral and weeping uncontrollably would add a dash of romantic intrigue to any memorial.

Who is she? Why is she so upset? Did the old man have a secret lover? And a buxom babe to boot? Oh, the stories would resonate any time your memory was discussed.

Or you could go the complete opposite direction and hint at altruistic devotions.

Think of the reaction if you had some humbly dressed pseudo-social worker show up and declare that you spent up to 40 hours a week working in the local soup kitchen.

"He swore me to secrecy," he'd say. "But he was there helping with the cooking, the serving, or just to be a strong shoulder to lean on with residents who needed a good listener. He was a true saint. He will be missed."

Imagine the impact on your legacy if your loved ones heard that line of bull. It would color their impressions of you for as long as they lived. And they'd feel stabs of pitiless guilt for all the times they accused you of being out drinking with your bar buddies night after night after night.

Take a wild guess as to the inspiration for that last one.

Other scenarios could include the appearance of an exotic, mixed-race prospective love child, a mysterious biographer, or a suspicious Russian spy.

Want to set off a belated panic among your greedy survivors?

Hire a spiffy industrialist to show up in a chauffeured limo to say he was a secret partner in a spectacular investment from years ago and had been curious to see how you'd spent your half of the fortune.

So, you see, you don't need to worry about a funeral that's boring or poorly attended.

You have it in your power to stage a funeral that will convince your survivors you were well-loved, you were generous and that the time you'd spent on earth was time well spent.

Of course, that's something that's always been within your power.

I guess it comes down to whether you want to enrich a guy like me or devote your days to enriching the whole world.

Chapter 5

I was 'Born' in Latrobe

My life's timeline is odd in that I don't count myself as having been born until I moved to right here in Latrobe.

I say I was born here because Latrobe and the people here are the reasons I finally came fully alive. It was here that I became who I am. It was here I learned through observation about right and wrong in the real world. It was here I learned how the telling of a colorful story, both clean and dirty, could transform a room into a place suddenly no one wanted to leave. Right here in Latrobe, I learned about the importance of friendship, loyalty, empathy and the dual values of hard work and hard play. It wasn't until I was seasoned here in Latrobe that vital parts of my personality — wit, perspective, authenticity — came alive and began to strut.

So, indeed, I declare I was born here.

But, like most western Pennsylvanian children of sports fans, I'd been here years before any of that happened.

Growing up in the South Hills of Pittsburgh in the 70's, my sports-mad father found ample reason to travel to Latrobe and the lovely Laurel Highlands at least four or five times a summer. The first was Steeler training camp at Saint Vincent. The Steelers have been coming to Latrobe for summer camp since 1965.

I still remember as a young boy the thrill of seeing Franco Harris, Jack Lambert and Terry Bradshaw and other Steeler Hall of

Famers on the steamy practice fields at Saint Vincent (and later as a resident hearing, seeing and verifying stories of Steeler exploits in our Latrobe bars).

The second reason was golfing at Champion Lakes Golf Club, one of Pennsylvania's finest public courses. It is owned by Pirate great Dick Groat. He was in the on-deck circle when Bill Mazeroski hit his historic Game 7 walk-off home run to beat the New York Yankees and was one of my Dad's favorite ball players. My brother Eric and I'd get a kick out of watching the old man float around the room after Groat would recognize him and say, "Hi, Paul! Great to see you!" I'd later see Groat often at Champion Lakes or parties of common friends and he'd say of my late father — he died in 2004 — "Nobody loved Champion Lakes more than Paul Rodell."

That's when it was my turn to float around the room.

But on those long-ago rides I'd mostly snooze for the first 45 minutes of the drive, but come alive when we'd crest U.S. Route 30 East where it passed the old landmark Mountain View Inn. There, just off in the distance like a Conga line of stubby exclamation points, were the weathered and ancient nubs of the Chestnut Ridge branch of the Allegheny Mountains. Living near the city sprawl, I could sense my eyes were feasting on a sylvan wonderland, a playground of waterfalls, abundant trout streams and wooded paths with ever-changing seasonal splendors. I remember looking at those mountains and wondering about the people lucky enough to live there. Certainly, they must be, I thought, very content with this fine place they called home.

In 1992, I found out for myself. Twenty-seven years later, so far, so good.

How did I wind up here?

My first job was as a general assignment reporter at the old Nashville Banner.

I loved Nashville and all the friends I made there, but I was making so little money that getting a pizza with pepperoni *and* sausage was my idea of a gaudy splurge. I believed I could do better.

And, man, I missed home. I missed my old friends, ethnic neighborhoods, the Black & Gold home teams and all the rambunctious men and women who made weekends such a giddy joy. I was among the first generations that moved away from Pittsburgh only to immediately boomerang back.

Born a yinzer and a yinzer's all you'll ever really be. I'm fine with that. I've done my fair share of traveling and to me nothing will ever top Pittsburgh, still a city you can really put your arms around. I vowed I'd never again reside more than an hour's drive from the fountain at Point State Park and I never have.

My 1989 boomerang led me to a regular job — my last regular job. I was 25. The skimpy resume, however, paid enormous dividends that to this day enrich my every waking moment. It all started when the *Tribune-Review* in Greensburg hired me to do front-page features.

It was there in the Greensburg office that I met and fell in love with a sultry beauty from the lifestyle department. Her name was Valerie Glenz. We initially bonded over our love for country music, which with Alan Jackson, Reba McIntire, Randy Travis and Garth Brooks especially was enjoying a commercial peak. When Val was given a Sunday column to comment on country news I suggested they call it, "Fiddlin' Around with Val!"

It's what I've been doing ever since. We have two daughters, Josie, 18, and Lucy, 13. Josie just became a freshman at Saint Vincent College. My plan is to have lunch with her every day, an ambition she cruelly mocks.

But fate's other arbitrary interjection led to a 30-year frolic that shows no signs of ceasing.

Fate led me to Latrobe.

I was inexplicably transferred from the main Greensburg office to the 2-man Latrobe bureau. It seemed like a step back, a demotion to the hinterlands where nothing really ever happened. I was told I'd be working with Paul Peirce. Prior to that Paul'd worked with a string of co-workers whose extracurricular interests did not necessarily merge with his.

Or as his wife Patti put it: "Before you got there, he used to always come home unhappy. Now he's always happy, but he's never home."

Paul was my introductory guide to all that mattered in Latrobe. He took me to the fun places, both the dive-y and the posh, and introduced me to the refined leaders and wily rascals. It was like they'd constructed in some secret lab my perfect drinking buddy, named him Paul and told us we were all on our own.

So by 1992, I had a loving wife and I had one truly great friend. I thought I had it all. Looking back, the best thing I had going for me, however, was a simple appreciation that I had all I'd ever need right here in Latrobe.

This became evident in 2002 when I refused a tempting offer to become a big shot in the New York magazine scene, a move that would have led to far more money and prestige than I was earning as a freelance writer in a town where big shot New Yorkers thought nothing ever happened. A supportive colleague of mine had secured me an offer to become a senior editor at Glamour magazine.

I remember hearing that and thinking, "… *senior … editor … Glamour … Well, there are three words I never thought anyone would ever apply to me.*"

I talked it over briefly with Val. Neither of us felt like the pros outweighed the cons. With one daughter and one on the way, we felt no need to uproot ourselves. We at the time had Casey, a boisterous golden retriever born with an innate love for chasing Frisbees and an ill-fated one for chasing skunks (note: that fable about tomato juice as skunk stink solvent? It is hooey).

Circumstances eventually did dictate a move. After 15 years in our quaint little Main Street starter home — its ceremonial name is, I swear, Fred Rogers Drive — it was time go. Another baby was on the way. It was time to move. But move where? Two free spirits who could live anywhere decided there was no real reason to leave Latrobe. Our new Latrobe house was just 0.7 miles from our old one.

It sure made sense to me.

Plus, there were still one or two interesting people in town we'd yet to meet.

Chapter 6

Colorful Neighbors

When I declare I was belatedly at the age of 25 born here, you might think my Latrobe "parents" were either Arnold Palmer or Fred Rogers, two monumental opinion-shapers who've inspired the ideals and personalities of impressionable young men and women from all over the world.

All through my early years, neither of these titans was on my radar. I'd hear rumors that one or the other had been seen dining at the Rainbow Inn or the Touchdown Club, but I had nothing to do with them. The men might as well have been ghosts they were so far out of my mortal reach. I never dreamed I'd have any personal contact with either of them. I failed to realize just how small a town Latrobe is. It's a place where eventually everybody meets everybody.

Want to know what was always within handy reach back in those days?

An ice-cold Rolling Rock beer!

That and lively conversation. From the church pews to the barstools, every seat seemed to be occupied by someone with something interesting to say and a colorful way to say it. The ones I met were bawdy, boisterous, opinionated, restless and could swing from rude to refined at the turn of a topic. To use an appropriate vulgarity, they were ballsy.

And those were just the babes!

Every one seemed to exude either joy or danger, rainbows or storm clouds. No one was ever overcast.

So if my Latrobe model teachers weren't Palmer and Rogers, who were they?

Two of them were Ned Nakles Sr. and Carl W. Kenly.

One name is now familiar to several generations of Greater Latrobe Senior High School students. He is universally remembered as one of Greater Latrobe's greatest advocates. The other is remembered only by devoted family and a dwindling number of aging inebriates. Me, I'll never forget him.

I choose to highlight Nakles and Kenly because they are particularly vibrant examples of the range, depth and sparkling vivacity of memorable characters you find in Latrobe.

There is a portrait of Ned in the high school Center for Student Creativity. Doubtless, hundreds of indifferent students pass it daily without paying it or its grinning subject the slightest attention. Me, every time I'm there, and I'm there often, I stop in front of his portrait to pay silent homage to one of the finest men I've ever known.

The portrait and hundreds of other works of art are there because Ned, who died in 1999, and his wife Barbara were driven by a tireless belief that every well-rounded life requires a mind-opening exposure to the fine arts. It is because of tangible and enduring support of families like the Nakleses that the Latrobe high school has an original art collection of more than 185 works that line the halls and corridors of the building. The collection is entirely student-selected, and, for the most part, student-purchased. It is one of the finest collections of 20th and 21st century Southwestern Pennsylvania art on display.

His son, Christopher, once told me growing up with Ned as his father was like being raised by Atticus Finch, the wise, warm and enduring scholar/warrior from "To Kill a Mockingbird." We sons of dead fathers tend to exaggerate and sanctify the memories of the flawed men who raised us. But with Chris the analogy is bullseye perfect in all respects but one: There's no record that Atticus ever bought anyone's lunch.

Ned bought lunch for everyone all the time. He did it routinely and joyfully.

We'd go to lunch nearly every day at Baldonieri's on Ligonier Street. The food was great. The chili had, not ground meat, but great chunks of tender roast beef in a savory stew, and they had a Cajun fish sandwich that was unequaled by many of its more famous French Quarter counterparts. But lunch at Baldonieri's would have been memorable even if the fare had not been.

It was because of the Ned-led conversation. We talked history, current events, sports, work and family and the soulful reasons why the former should never be permitted to take precedence over the latter.

Without any of us even being aware of the education, he was tutoring us. Then he'd ask for the bill — admonishing us, too, that over-tipping a friendly waitress was a virtue.

Sometimes he'd go even further. He once offered to pay for me to go to law school, a generosity I hastily and foolishly declined. I was committed to being a writer (idiot). I sometimes wonder how different my life would be today had I accepted. I'd likely today be a successful attorney or — who knows? — maybe even a judge.

I don't say that out of arrogance, but it is indicative of one of the many tangible ways he's still touching the future. He saw things in people we were incapable of seeing in ourselves. He did so by investing in things like people, hope and optimism. Those are the cornerstones that make any community — any person — thrive.

When Ned died in 1999 at the age of 68, I was flattered to be asked to contribute to the page 1 *Tribune-Review* obit with my buddy Paul. It included the cliche tributes you see and hear at the passing of any great man or woman. He was kind, civil, funny, generous, etc. I liked the part about how he cherished his home library in which he'd amassed a collection of 10,000 rare books, but not without humane perspective. "If the house was on fire," he'd said, "and I could only save either 10 rare books or save the little dog, I'd save the dog."

I liked the part that pointed out he was so nimble-minded he could over one lunch cite quotes from the Bible, William Shakespeare and TV junkman Fred Sanford and have them all make conversational sense.

You don't find people that well-rounded, that wise and exuberant, in just any old town.

But you can find them in Latrobe.

My other bookend designate of greatness will surprise people who assume greatness should be more refined, more dashing, more eligible for a marble bust presented in some hero-lined hall. And Carl Kenly was none of those things. A retired WW II Marine who served in the Panama Canal Zone, he was maybe the most profane and entertaining man I've ever known. He had the rowdy kind of charisma that often inspired young men like I was back then to instinctively follow them into battle.

But there were no battles in Latrobe so Paul and I instinctively followed him into every bar in town. He knew everybody and knew just about everything there was to know about them. He had a breathtaking honesty about being human and about human beings. He could be very offensive to people who prefer subtlety and dainty tact.

I never once called him Carl. To us, he was always The Snapper, so named because he could so explosively snap his fingers in percussive salute or hambone dance routine when he thought things were getting boring, a situation I never once detected in his presence.

The first time I met The Snapper it was to borrow a plunger. Such were the indignities of remote bureau life that the cranky toilet often malfunctioned. This happened on my very first day there. B.C. Kenly's, named after his son Bill and daughter-in-law Cheryl, was one door down the sidewalk from the office, near enough as we later discovered that if the door to our office and the doors to the bar were open we could hear the office phone ring from our barstools. Paul and I often put this geographic audio quirk to good use.

Snapper ran the bar for his son from 1 to 7 p.m. I walked in at 2 p.m. and, with some hemming and hawing explained my predicament. He put me at ease, sort of, by graphically pointing out every person must yield to the biological function that led to the trouble. Then he went and got the plunger.

He extended it to me, but then pulled it back as if he were protecting a priceless violin.

"You ever use a plunger before?"

I told him I had.

"You know, there's only two things you need to know about the plunger. One, the end of the plunger with the rubber suction cup is the end that goes in the toilet and, two, never ever put the part that goes into the toilet in your mouth."

It didn't matter if it was a bank teller, a cop, or a young reporter, Snapper saw every interaction with his fellow man as an opportunity for mischief.

It's a challenge to write about a man so profane, so exuberantly filthy, in a book about Mister Rogers' Neighborhood, but Snapper lived here, too. He's as much a part of the Real Neighborhood as Fred himself. And he was adamant about who belonged and who didn't. And he could be crafty about applying the rules.

Like other bartenders, he'd card youths he considered too unseasoned or too cheerful. Back then, being too cheerful in Kenly's was considered suspicious behavior. Often the would-be customers would eagerly produce their IDs and chirp about their legality.

Snapper never even peeked at the licenses. "Get out," he'd command. "You gotta be 30 to drink here."

I'll always remember him telling with diabolical glee the story of the prank that almost led to the untimely holiday homicide of Stan, the security guard at the old Teledyne Vasco plant just outside of town. He spent the day before Thanksgiving telling dozens of co-workers the owners had sprung for free turkeys and all they had to do was ask Stan at the entrance security gate to give them one.

He then sealed poor Stan's doom by embroidering the fib with a string of malicious whoppers.

"Now, last year they busted Stan (lie) denying he had any turkeys (lie) and keeping them all for himself (lie). So if you ask him for your turkey he'll deny knowing anything about any free turkeys (true!). Don't let him get away with it (call 911!)."

It's my understanding prayers of Thanksgiving around Stan's dinner table the next day were extra heartfelt. Stan was lucky to be alive.

When I asked Snapper why he'd play a prank that could cause an unsuspecting man so much duress, he said, "I thought it would be helpful for Stan to learn to think on his feet. Plus, I thought it would be funny."

I couldn't argue with his logic.

So those are just two examples of the kind of men you'd meet here in Mister Rogers Real Neighborhood. They're unique in some ways, typical in others.

They're just two of my favorites.

Chapter 7

Were Arnold & Fred Pals?

I shudder to think the snub was deliberate, but there was never any Arnold Palmer in "Mister Rogers Neighborhood." There was a Lady Elaine Fairchild, a Henrietta Pussycat and a Daniel Striped Tiger, all from the Land of Make-Believe. Real-life celebrity guests included chef Julia Child, singer Tony Bennett, Science Guy Bill Nye, bodybuilder ("Incredible Hulk") Lou Ferrigno and gorilla Koko The, er, Gorilla.

But no Arnold Palmer.

The show that featured a make-believe puppet King never once in 895 episodes over 31 years had time for The King, the confidant of true royalty and presidents alike and a benchmark for sportsmanship and fair play. Palmer was arguably one of the most popular men on the planet from 1960 through his 2016 death (and beyond). And of all the famous guests visiting Fred in "Mister Rogers' Neighborhood" Arnold Palmer would have been the only one who was an actual neighbor.

Imagine the cheery fanfare of Fred Rogers introducing Arnold Palmer to his impressionable TV friends. He could have been nostalgic. He could have referenced old teachers. He could have saved a fortune on guest mileage reimbursement.

But it never happened. Not even once.

Rogers and Palmer, two generation-transcending icons around

the globe, were born less than 18 months and just a few miles apart. They knew the same families, had the same teachers, as children watched the same Fourth of July fireworks and perhaps — who knows? — sat on the same Santa's lap as they shared their Christmas lists.

In fact, throughout their lives, both of which involved ample service to Latrobe, the pair acted like the other didn't exist. You could say one of their closest associations was Deacon Palmer taught both men how to golf (one turned out to be a much better student than the other).

Search the internet using any variety of keywords you like and you'll be unable to find a single picture of Arnold Palmer and Fred Rogers doing anything together.

The pair in the mid-90's were jointly honored by the chamber of commerce, perhaps the only time they ever shared a dais (I found nothing on the internet and was restricted by deadline tyrannies from deeper digs).

Was there a sibling sort of rivalry between the two over who had bragging rights in their small hometown?

Indeed, there was.

There was at least in one direction. It may have been momentary, it may have been an inadvertent slip, but it was evident even to an unflinching admirer like me.

It was the summer of 2004. Palmer had just been awarded the Presidential Medal of Freedom. I was at his office to interview him on an unrelated matter, but wanted to start the banter with what I thought would be some mood-lightening flattery.

"Congratulations, Mr. Palmer, on the Presidential Medal of Freedom!"

He beamed. He was justifiable proud to be one of fewer than 700 Americans deemed worthy of the exalted honor. So proud, I didn't realize my follow-up remark would be an affront to one of the most competitive men to have ever lived.

"What's that say for Latrobe? Not one but two winners of the nation's highest civilian award. Cool, huh!"

It was like I'd told him he'd played the wrong ball on the final hole on Sunday at the Masters. His whole demeanor changed.

"Who else?" he asked.

"Why, Fred Rogers was awarded his in 2002."

"He was? Two years ago?"

Yes, sir.

It wasn't anger, but his face betrayed an emotion more visceral than miffed disappointment. The best word to describe it was one Mr. Rogers would never use.

Mr. Palmer was pissed.

To this day, I tell that story to anyone interested in hearing just how competitive a man Palmer was. He was upset that someone else from town by two years beat him to one of America's highest honors and not only was that man a good and decent man, a worthy recipient, but that man was Fred Rogers.

His reaction, brief as it was, was purely irrational, but that was a component of his greatness.

"Platoon" was the 1986 Oliver Stone Oscar-winning film about a young Vietnam War soldier (Charlie Sheen) who is circumstantially forced to choose between the hardened and cynical Staff Sgt. Barnes (played by Tom Berenger) or the more sweetly tempered and idealistic Sgt. Elias (Willem Dafoe).

Mayhem ensues.

It has always seemed to me that Latrobe was years ago challenged to make a similar choice with its personality at stake.

I contend it never could make up its mind and simply settled for the best of both.

In death, Palmer and Rogers share something more permanent, more concrete, than anything they ever did in life. It was 2015 when PennDOT road crews began repairing the State Route 982 bridge over U.S. Route 30. PennDOT considers it enough of a landmark they've opted to pay the extra dough to inscribe the bridge siding with tributes to Rogers and Palmer.

The west side says, "It's A Beautiful Day in the Neighborhood;" the east, "A Greater Latrobe Area Legend • Arnold Palmer."

One side leads north to downtown Latrobe; the other south to the world beyond.

As I said, there is no indication, anecdotal or otherwise, that either of these two giants disliked the other. I've heard nothing of the sort. To the contrary, there is ample evidence they were mutual admirers of all they did in the different fields in which they flourished.

But there is no evidence of any genuine kinship between two truly great men who grew up to share vast global appeal known to only a rarified few.

The neighbors just weren't all that neighborly.

Life Lesson on ...

Friendship

More evidence that I deserve my "All Star Dad" mug came in 2016 when I was chatting with our then-10-year-old on the walk home from the school bus stop. I asked if she'd yet made any new friends in the new school year.

She had not.

She then out-of-the-blue revealed she'd two years ago heeded some of my keystone advice and that it had really paid off.

"Do you remember telling me the way to make friends is to ask strangers if they want to be friends?"

I did. I for years have told my daughters as they depart for the first day of school that this was the day they could meet someone who'll be their very best friend for the rest of their lives.

It's a beautiful sentiment because it's true. Every time we step outside the house we have an opportunity to make a brand-new friend. Think about that and open your eyes to the possibility. It'll enhance your every human encounter.

What can I say? Some days I channel Fred Rogers.

As the girls got older I began amending the sentiment to include the fact that, this being modern America, any time they step outside they could also intercept a bullet so be sure to duck anytime you hear gunfire.

What can I say? Some days I channel Chris Rock.

Two years after she'd first heard the advice, Lucy told me that was how she'd met Aryn and Ally.

"I went up to them and said, 'My name is Lucy. Do you want to be friends?' They said yes and today they're my best friends."

I was blown away.

For many years, darling Lucy was what many adults describe as shy.

"She's shy."

They'd say it in a voice that sounded like they were diagnosing leprosy.

I treasure shy people and am daily thrilled I had a role in raising one of them.

Knowing her as I do, I'd say it was just a matter of time until her confidence caught up with her vivacious personality.

Way too many adults — predominantly males — have the exact opposite problem.

I'm one of them.

We're confident. We brag. We bluster. We blog. We shout to the world we have really big hands.

But for a moment think of the courage of that quiet little 8-year-old daring to approach playground strangers to humbly request their friendship. Remember how painful any rejection is at that age? She's risking humiliation, taunting and stony indifference.

Shy?

The kid could be on SEAL Team 6.

The rise in online isolation saddens me for the future. We're so wedded to our virtual diversions we're blind to the chances to make authentic friends.

We could learn a lot from kids like Lucy.

Keep the phone in the pocket. Make eye contact. And be confident you're offering for free something every single human being wants and needs.

Asking anyone if they want to be your friend is so disarming it infuses the brain with joyful potential. It hints at Tom-and-Huck-like adventures to be. It opens the possibility of a lifetime of laughter and inside jokes in rooms full of strangers.

It's utterly euphoric.

"Hello. My name is Chris. Will you be my friend?"

That humble little request is the prelude to the fact I'll soon consider you an eligible source for me to bum money.

That's what friends are for, too!

Chapter 8

Monuments to Fred

It was to his legions of admirers frustrating but, perhaps, fitting that it took worthy statues honoring Fred Rogers so long to land. Nothing about Fred was ever rushed so why would something designed to be forever stationary? Oddly enough, of the three prominent western Pennsylvania statues honoring Rogers, the one that's been on display the longest has Jurassic roots, so you could argue artist Karen Howell had a 66 million year head start. It makes sense if you figure she had the most difficult task.

While the others were asked to make statues of Fred that conveyed the realities of Fred — smiling, gentle, eager to share understanding and comfort — Howell was commissioned to take one of the most vicious, bloodthirsty and historically crabby creatures and make it appear cuddly to kids.

Yes, Howell had to make a Tyrannosaurus Fred.

How'd she do it?

"Well, you start by dressing it up in sneakers and a red cardigan sweater," she says.

The project was initially part of the Carnegie Museum of Natural History's DinoMite Days from 2003 when the organization funded 100 artists to create and unleash dino-inspired works of art spread throughout Pittsburgh. The intention was to entertain residents and remind everyone that Pittsburgh is home to the third-largest collection of authentic dinosaur bones in the world.

City of Chompions!

Howell says she was careful to customize details lest they frighten children. "I converted the front teeth so they looked more human, more Fred-like, so the regular T-Rex teeth wouldn't scare the kids." The teeth of Fredosaurus look like they're more apt to snap up a stack of s'mores than any stegosaurus.

Other uniquely Fred flourishes include the dinosaur holding Henrietta Pussycat in his right arm; King Friday XIII in his left. The trolley, too, makes a beguiling appearance, fixed as it is about halfway up the beast's tail.

Circumstances, logistical and larcenous, have led to several repairs and one complete refurbish when it was moved to its current location outside Fred Rogers Productions, 2100 Wharton St., on Pittsburgh's South Side.

"The puppets were stolen on Labor Day weekend before an auction and the trolley fell off during St. Patrick's Day when a woman tried to climb on the back of the dinosaur. Public art takes a lot of abuse!"

Signs warning of security cameras — "HANDS OFF I BITE!" You can take my picture, because I'm taking yours" — now discourage vandals.

But nothing can be done to discourage online critics prone to cheap shots against the sit-down statue that stands out for its prominence, scale and artistic endorsement of the gentle subject himself. Located on the banks of the Allegheny River and overlooking the city he loved, the $3 million "Tribute to Children" was unveiled in 2009 and has been a target of online critics ever since.

- *"If a mud monster mated with The Thing from the Fantastic Four, this would be the result. The toothy grin is kind of creepy."* Frank A., Pittsburgh
- *"What a remarkably ugly statue... did a child make it with Play-Doh?" JamesA546, Windsor, Ontario*
- *"If I were a kid, seeing this statue would make me afraid to watch Mr. Rogers." Mitchell H. Pittsburgh*

How can fans of Mr. Rogers respond to heartfelt and lavish tribute to Mr. Rogers in the coarse sort of terms that would so dismay Mr. Rogers?

Let's take a step back. The work was commissioned by Mellon family heiress and Rogers' pal Cordelia Scaife May. In 2005, the year of her death, May was recognized as the single most generous person in the United States. Her charitable donations for the year were almost one-tenth of the $4.3 billion donated by the nation's leading philanthropists. And she wasn't scattergun about her largesse, especially one involving a friend.

Knowing Fred would have wanted it, she awarded the $3-million commission to Robert Berks. It was Berks who did a beloved Albert Einstein statue in D.C. Rogers was so enamored of the Berks' Einstein he is said to have stopped to enjoy solitary contemplation whenever he was in Washington.

The statue is located so it can overlook the river, a nod to Fred's love of swimming. It says something positive about Pittsburgh's inclusiveness that a statue honoring a gentle man renown for mannerly kindness is in the same neighborhood as men renowned for brute toughness. The statue is a long post route from the south end zone of Heinz Field, home of the 6-time Super Bowl champion Pittsburgh Steelers.

As for the discordant snark, a local author whose book celebrates the city's eclectic appeals says, meh, criticism schmiticism.

"I like the way he's posed. It's like Mr. Rogers is watching over the city," says Rossilynne Skena Culgan, author of "100 Things to do in Pittsburgh Before You Die," Reedy Press, 2019. "His statue has a really special place in my heart. It's very comforting. I know many people feel the same as I do."

In 2015, a sound system was added and comes with a 29-song playlist of Fred's greatest hits.

She's heard and is dismissive of the criticism: "I've heard people refer to the statue as 'lumpy' or 'muddy,' but I like the statue's appearance. I'm no art critic, but this textured style is emblematic of the artist's work, and I quite like it. For Mr. Rogers, in particular, I think it's a perfect fit because the style has always reminded me of a carefree finger painting."

It's unlikely you'll hear any pointed criticism of Jon Hair's landmark statue because his is the Fred Rogers statue that everyone will look at and instantly say, "Hey, that's Fred Rogers!"

Hair is a statue-maker of such accomplishment and virtuosity someone should really think about making a statue out of him. Just not yet. He's too dynamic a person to pause and pose. His statues are stationary, but the artist has spent his life in constant motion. As a youth, he was a skilled-enough drummer to have jammed with Jimi Hendrix. For real.

And, oh, the metaphorical company he keeps.

He's caroused with John Coltrane, Mark Twain and Rosa Parks; he's broken bread with Marie Curie, Galileo, Sacajawea and Teddy Roosevelt. And don't get him started about the times he spent with that well-known party animal Mother Teresa.

"I like to tell people I have kids on 38 campuses around the country," says Hair, a Cedar Rapids, Iowa, native who after a nomadic life eventually opened a St. Petersburg, Florida, studio. He didn't begin sculpting until he was 50 and in the 19 years since has unveiled 110 monumental works. He's done sculptures for the cities of Beijing and Shanghai, the U.S. Olympic Committee, the U.S. Air Force, and the Emmy's Hall of Fame.

So what was it like working with a subject as benign and gracious as Fred Rogers?

"It was tough," he said. He was unable to find a suitable profile shot that would enhance his intuitive grasp of the subject's appearance. All the pictures submitted to Hair were straight on. He needed perspective.

It was maybe the first time anyone said a situation would have improved had Fred Rogers been more two-faced. But the sculptor persevered and so nailed the likeness of Rogers that upon seeing it, Fred's late sister, Nancy Rogers Crozier, kissed the statue's cheek and exclaimed, "It IS my brother."

"I love Mr. Rogers," Hair says. "I wanted to make sure he was perfect because people have such an emotional connection to him. I have great empathy for children who come from challenging backgrounds. It was important to get him just right. He's still making a difference in so many lives."

Howell, Berks and Hair work in different ways and with different media. But they all start their art with the elements Fred nurtured in children and the grownups who inspire them.

They all start with heart and soul.

Chapter 9

Fred's Hero

We build monuments to celebrate our reverence for Fred Rogers and all he means to the world. We do so in the hopes that future generations will emulate his deeds and, we hope, make the world a better place.

But if Fred had any say in the matter, it's likely he'd politely refuse the honor and advise us, friends, if you're interested in honoring a man worthy of emulation, build one in honor of Jim Stumbaugh.

Because without the unsung classmate, the world may have never heard of Fred Rogers.

Dirk Richwine, Latrobe class of '78, is today director of the Denver-based National Recreation and Parks Association, a non-profit dedicated to enhancing community quality of life through foundational play. He remains a devotee of Latrobe and always includes Stumbaugh in his canon of heroes.

Why Stumbaugh?

"Because I'm convinced without Jim Stumbaugh the world would never have heard of Fred Rogers," he says. "Jim Stumbaugh changed Fed Rogers so Fred Rogers could change the world."

It's difficult to imagine how shy and sheltered Rogers was as a boy, and how those characteristics coupled with his perceived family wealth led to him being tortured. And if torture seems unduly harsh even for extreme bullying, understand that Richwine heard from

Rogers' contemporaries in his family that Rogers had known "safe houses" to which he could run for protection when the wolves began to circle.

"Those were the exact words — 'safe house,'" he says. "His mother knew he was being bullied and she had a series of homes on the way home from school where he knew he could run when the bullies were after him. I don't think many people realize how difficult his childhood was. Jim Stumbaugh changed all that practically overnight."

One of the most popular kids in school, Stumbaugh suffered a football injury that led to hospitalization where Fred's mother worked. She sensed he was the kind of boy who could help her troubled son. She arranged for Fred to take him his assignments in the hopes the popular boy would see the good in Fred. Her plan worked beyond her wildest dreams. As Fred recalled it years later:

"There he was, probably the best-known, smartest, most active person in our class and he welcomed me day after day. And what's more, he seemed to want to get to know me. I learned to trust him and told him some of my deepest feelings ... By the time he got out of the hospital and back to school, he was telling all of his friends that 'that Rogers kid is OK.' In fact, he quietly included me in everything he thought I'd like."

There's a hindsight poignancy to that humble admission that practically sheds tears. The transformation in Rogers was breathtaking.

He went nearly overnight from being picked on to being popular. Rogers went on to become student council president and editor of the yearbook "largely because I had somebody who believed in me and wasn't afraid to say so."

The pair remained close throughout their lives and when Rogers heard his old friend was battling cancer, he flew to visit Stumbaugh at his North Carolina home even though Rogers himself was at the time hobbling on crutches from an ankle injury. And when Stumbaugh died, one of the speakers who accepted an invitation to eulogize the unheralded former school star with the generous heart was Fred Rogers, a man who'd be eulogized by presidents and adoring souls from around the world.

Consider, Stumbaugh's was not some fabled random act of kindness. He wasn't acting on an intuition that one day Fred Rogers would become famous and cite him as the reason it all came to be. He wasn't being opportunistic.

He was being human.

"What Stumbaugh did was allow Fred Rogers to finally be himself and when he showed the world he was the whole world came to realize he was something magnificent."

He is a true role model for Richwine, who says he is inspired by the hometown story at least once a week.

"Jim Stumbaugh is the whole cornerstone to the success of Fred Rogers," he says. "It's because of him I view it as my responsibility to help as many young people as I can. I consider it a privilege to plow the road and make the path easier for the next group of leaders. And that's all because of Jim Stumbaugh and what he did for Fred and thus the world."

Being Fred is unattainable to most of us. We're busy. We have tempers. We're human.

It's a little more realistic to be someone's Jim Stumbaugh.

And if you can't be Stumbaugh, then there is still a critical role in making this world a better place.

You can be Dirk Richwine.

Life Lesson on ...

Bullying

I guess they were what you'd call cool girls. Cool for 15. They were each attractive in their own way, supremely self-assured and clumped up all together in a little clique by the side of the high school pool.

There were four of them. Their practice started in 20 minutes. It was a typical after-school swim club practice, which meant I was sitting in the stands enjoying my book but attentive to what was going on.

I'd look up from the Churchill biography to make eye contact with my darling little minnow, then 9 years old, when she'd glance in my direction and smile while waiting her turn to ascend the diving platform.

I'd smile back.

I love her with my whole heart.

She is surrounded by other similar-sized boys and girls and one older boy who towers over them in size and maturity. He is bigger even than most of the adults.

I know nothing of his situation but am observant enough to speculate.

He is unfit and has been told competitive swimming will dramatically change his body shape. He is eager to do this so he submits to the adolescent indignity of standing in line with children who are roughly half his age and size.

He's trying so hard, but the changes he's seeking — and this is a lesson some of us never learn — take time and dedication. I admire him and the parents who gave him this wise counsel.

I cannot gauge his desperation to be liked or accepted for who he is, but few are the junior high school students who revel in being all alone in what for many are the most difficult years of their foundational lives.

He emerges from the pool with great difficulty. His muscles aren't strong enough to lift his full girth from the water and he just sort of inelegantly flops out and unfolds his frame to its full 6-foot-1 height.

He has a shy smile as he walks toward the cool girls right in front of me. He makes direct eye contact with each, comes to a stop, and chirps out one word in a bird-like voice.

"Hello."

They pretend they don't hear him.

He says it again.

"Hello."

It is as if he doesn't exist.

He walks away. The girls give each other nervous glances. Who does he think he is?

But the boy is blessed with persistence. He makes another lap, struggles out of the water and again approaches.

"Hello."

No reaction.

It happened just like that three more times.

"Hello."

Nothing.

He walks away and this time he does not return. He is defeated. The girls share mean little smiles. And my heart breaks.

For him, sure. What happened to him was tough to watch, let alone endure. But it also breaks for the cool girls.

Because I have been cursed with prophesy. I can see the future.

The hair-twirling blonde will be the prettiest girl in high school. The attention she gets for her fine appearance will convince her youthful looks will never fade. About this, she is mistaken. In 10 years she will be married to her high school sweetheart, a popular football player. He will spend the next 20 years cheating on her with a succession of younger, prettier girls until divorce lawyers are summoned. She will spend long hours looking in the mirror and realizing every day for the rest of her life it's all been downhill since the 2021 senior prom.

The one with the cute pony tail will enjoy a successful administrative career at a nearby university. She'll find satisfaction in her job, but she'll wonder if something's missing. The first marriage didn't work out. He was a drinker, a mean one. She spends long nights at the office intermittently checking match.com profiles of men who invite prospective dates to come over and cook them dinner. She remembers the one guy who asked if she was good with laundry. She gets together with friends for lunch once a month. They sit around bitching about what jerks men are.

The perky girl will get married and raise a family. She will love her children with fierce devotion, but as the kids get older and find their own diversions she will wonder what happened to the man she married. He's so distant. He comes home from work and turns on the Penguin games and never even asks about her day. How could he be so indifferent? Doesn't he know how much it hurts to be ignored?

The fourth girl will get everything she's ever dreamed of. She will marry a kind, handsome man. He'll be a good provider, attentive to her emotional needs and will relish spending time with their bright, beautiful children, whom they will raise with love and wisdom.

And some night, many years from now, she will recall how cruelly she treated that awkward open-faced boy who just wanted someone to acknowledge his existence. And there in that bed she'll share with the man she loves, she will shed tears of soulful regret.

"How," she'll wonder, "could I have been so mean? What was I thinking?"

I should have said something about simple manners, about our common humanity.

I should have said, "C'mon, just say hello. You don't have to kiss the kid. Just be nice. Be human. Show him a little kindness today and, guaranteed, 30 years from now he'll make your day by telling you at your high school reunion he remembers how sweet you were that day when he felt he was all alone.

"That kid could grow up to be someone special. But you need to understand being nice now will make a difference in your futures, too. You have a chance to make the whole world better and you're letting it slip away."

To my everlasting disgust, I said nothing. I am a coward.

What's the worst that could have happened?

That these cool 15-year-old girls would have snickered at my little lecture? That they'd have ignored me?

I like to think at least I'd have been in good company.

Chapter 10

Joy Riding the Idlewild Trolley

The summer I was teaching my darling teen how to drive my crappy 2007 Saturn Vue, the one with 207,800 miles on it, she responded with a very Mr. Rogers gesture. She offered to reciprocate by letting me take the wheel of something she drove.

If you think this means I got to take a drive-way spin on her Big Wheel you don't know my daughter.

No, I got to drive Mister Rogers' trolley through the real land of Make-Believe. And I didn't have to go to the trouble of miniaturizing to fit through the tunnels.

Josie from 2016 through 2019 worked summers at the Idlewild and Soak Zone about five miles east of Latrobe on U.S. Route 30. The park has multiple times been awarded the *Amusement Today* trade magazine's "Golden Ticket" for World's Best Children's Park. A big reason for the accolades was the Fred Rogers-conceived "Neighborhood of Make-Believe," updated to "Daniel Tiger's Neighborhood" in 2015 to, as press releases at the time said so the attraction would remain "relevant." I contend the marketing department confused "relevant" for "current."

Fred Rogers will be relevant for as long as there are children.

Josie started her Idlewild career scooping Dippin' Dots, the "ice cream of the future" for, I guess, people for whom actual ice cream just isn't hip enough. But in '17 she was promoted — not into the future — but back in time.

She'd drive the iconic "Land of Make-Believe" trolley, built to scale to resemble the actual one Fred conducted on his show. It charmingly winds through the woods at about 4 mph past show landmarks where she bantered with various characters via script and taped dialogue.

It was a huge honor, I told her. "To many guests, that trolley *is* Idlewild," I said. "It symbolizes what that park is all about."

It was the wrong thing to say to a teenage employee eager to leap into the next phase of her life. The things that spring to her mind are the heat, the crowds, the surly parents and the hours spent marooned on the trolley while her friends are doing fun stuff.

"You're not trolley driver," I say. "You make sad people happy. You're a magician! You're part of history!"

Jennifer Sopko agrees — and she ought to know. She's the author of "Idlewild: History and Memories of Pennsylvania's Oldest Amusement Park (The History Press, 2018).

She said the "Make-Believe" ride is unique in that it was designed wholly by Rogers himself with the deliberate intention of eschewing craven commercialism.

"He was insistent 'Mister Rogers' Neighborhood of Make-Believe' would reflect the values of his long-running television show many parents and children loved, rather than becoming just another product," she says. "From developing the concept of the life-sized trolley ride through the Neighborhood to writing the script, composing the music and recording the voices for all of the animatronic characters, he was involved every step of the way."

It's one of the splendors of a park so intimate and inviting the whole place feels like one big leafy neighborhood. Built in 1878 by Mellon family scions (old money descendants of Andrew and R.K. Mellon still call the Laurel Highlands home), the park was initially a picnic and campground. Ownership planted 10,000 shrubs the first year and maintained an aggressive tree-planting program throughout the park's existence making Idlewild a shady respite during even the most stifling summer days.

And the park's popularity continued to grow right along with the trees.

It was in 1988 that park officials decided to replace a zoo element with a major new attraction.

"However," Sopko writes, "true to Idlewild's philosophy, it was not a monster theme ride. Instead, it was a ride designed to instill good feelings and self-worth in its young patrons."

That meant it was a Fred Rogers attraction, a life-size trolley ride through the land of Make-Believe. Idlewild's leadership, Keith Hood, Harry Henninger and Carl Hughes, met Rogers over lunch and in 30 minutes the parties agreed to a handshake deal that would secure the future of the $1-million ride.

Passengers board the trolley in the real world and are transported to the Land of Make-Believe where King Friday XIII asks them to on their journey invite show characters to a castle hug-and-song party. So riders in unison stop and urge all the characters to "Come along, come along to the castle hug-and-song."

For Rogers, it was like coming home. He'd spent many idyllic summer days there and in 1994 told local historian E. Kay Myers, "I think Idlewild is the most naturally beautiful amusement park in the world."

It's a place he never outgrew. Sean Myers recalls being a lifeguard at the Soakzone wave pool in the '90's. The park was closed on Mondays, but his supervisor asked if anyone wanted to snag some easy duty extra hours. Mister Rogers was coming to the neighborhood.

"It was just for him and his family," Myers said. "I was sitting at the life guard chair right near the entrance. I remember he came right up and said hello. He was as nice as could be. He asked my name and how I enjoyed the job. Two days later I got a card in the mail from him saying how much he enjoyed meeting me."

Keith Hood was the park general manager from 1978-2002

and oversaw the attraction's development. He said "I think Fred Rogers' guiding hand is why the attraction has been so successful and beloved by so many people. He took a key element of his show — a visit to the fictional Neighborhood of Make-Believe — and made it interactive. Kids would be able to meet the characters from the show and interact with them by inviting them to a "Hug and Song" party at King Friday XIII's castle. They became a part of the world they watched every day on television."

The trolley transports up to 40 guests and was commissioned by the Indianapolis Zoo from the Gales Creek Enterprises, based in Forest Grove, Oregon. Built to be drawn by horses through the zoo, the trolley proved too heavy for the task. So it was refitted with engines and sold to Idlewild.

Like Mr. Rogers himself, it's nothing flashy.

Just a little joy ride on a ride that's brought joy to generations.

Life Lesson on ...

Fatherhood

About the only ground we didn't cover in a glorious 2014 winter day of father-daughter bonding was what she wants to be when she grows up. We didn't get to that, I think, because I was consumed by the self-epiphany that I had finally figured out what I want to be when I grow up.

I'm wanna be a ski instructor!

In fact, I guess I already am one. I just didn't know it.

I hadn't skied in 20 years. We have friends that used to have a great cozy chalet in Lake Placid, N.Y. We'd go every February. Lake Placid was the site of the winter Olympics in 1932 and, of course, 1980, when it hosted "The Miracle on Ice."

I'd never been much for winter vacations, preferring to visit Key West, Myrtle Beach and other places that required less, not more, clothing.

But idyllic Lake Placid in winter was a revelation. It's a wonderful town and I really loved immersing myself in a week of skiing. So much skiing in so little time has a way of making one competent quick.

Still, when Josie, 13, expressed an interest in learning to ski, I was ready to dodge. I figured she'd be better off taking a beginner's class from a certified instructor than learning from me.

And maybe she would have. We'll never know.

Because I undertook the task myself after learning an hour-long lesson at Hidden Valley would cost $82.

Eighty-two dollars an hour?

That's just a bit less than what I earned in all of 2009.

I could have gotten her a golf lesson from a prestigious country club professional for that much. And hitting a golf ball is far more difficult than skiing down a hill. Learning to golf requires touch, hand/eye coordination, concentration, balance, footwork, imagination, etc.

Learning to ski requires a base appreciation for the immutable role gravity plays in our daily lives.

What goes up (on a chair lift), must come down (on its butt).

That's why after about 10 minutes of primitive instruction, I took her on the four-seat chair lift to the very top of the mountain and basically just gave her a gentle shove.

I think someone making $82 an hour would feel obliged to over-earn his or her money by making a simple undertaking complicated.

We eventually made it down the beginner's trails clear to what I remember they used to call the "bunny slope." I don't think they call it that anymore, leading me to believe someone took offense, either a sensitive beginner or a really literate bunny.

It was useful, but I think what made me such a great teacher was giving her right away the opportunity to embrace the euphoria of overcoming fear that makes skiing so much fun.

She got to ride the chair lift. She got to revel in the splendors of being up at the top of a mountain in a snow storm.

It's all very exhilarating.

I was very pleased with how quickly I was able to pick it all back up. I'm confident I could have done all the black diamonds with skill and swagger.

But it was not to be.

Nope, as ski instructor I had to toddle along with my little darling. We were never more than 20 feet from one another. We went on all the trails, rode all the lifts and spent about six hours on the slopes. Just the two of us.

Experts swear biological imperatives mean I'll soon lose my little teenager for the next five or six years. She won't want anything to do with me. I'm sure at least some degree of that's bound to happen.

But on this day she was all mine.

And she did great.

She learned how to turn by shifting her weight, she learned how to control her speed by pizza-slice snow ploughing, and she learned the euphoric feeling of evading a fall to go faster on snow than she'd ever imagined.

She learned all that in about 30 minutes of casual instruction spread out over one great day.

And I learned something, too.

I learned the best part about being a freebie ski instructor to someone you love is all the soulful stuff you do between when you're trying to teach someone how to ski.

Chapter 11

Lah-Trobe or LAYtrobe?

The most common question people ask when they find out you're from Latrobe is, "So what's Arnold Palmer really like?" An in-depth answer to that question is further on in this book.

That means the second most common question people ask when they find out you're from Latrobe is, "So is it Latrobe or is it Latrobe?" Phonetically-speaking, they're asking is it Lah-trobe or is it LAY-trobe?

My scripted answer for that one is satisfying only to connoisseurs of small town snark. "To me," I say, "it's always been LAY-trobe because Lah-trobe sounds like a bistro on the banks of the Seine where chablis-sipping sophisticates nibble on biscotti. And anyone who's ever been to LAY-trobe knows LAY-trobe ain't gay Paree."

I think my answer captures the spirit of Latrobe — gritty, unpretentious, a little down & dirty. Why I felt this should be emphasized over Latrobe's culture, philanthropy and artistry is a matter for the pop psychiatrists.

LAY-trobe or Lah-trobe?

If you believe the results of a highly unscientific on-line poll conducted on the "You Know You're From Latrobe If ..." Facebook page, the locals in a landslide, 75 percent, say it's LAY-trobe.

Dennis Charlesworth has business cards proclaiming he's Latrobe's "Self-Appointed, Unofficial & International Ambassador."

A 1969 Latrobe graduate and a current resident of Covington, Louisiana, Charlesworth spent a career in human relations and spends much of his time extolling to strangers the proud virtues of his hometown.

Latrobe is his handy icebreaker in every conversation and it's always, "Hi, I'm Dennis. I'm from LAY-trobe, Pennsylvania." He has a Schnauzer rescue dog he named Arnie he takes with him on cheer visits to schools, nursing homes and veterans hospitals. He says Arnie is "real lady's man who loves meeting people."

He's talking about the dog here, although some confusion is inevitable.

"I tell stories about Arnold Palmer, talk about the banana split," he says. "LAY-trobe has something everyone can connect with. The other day I was taking Arnie to a nursing home and started telling a woman about LAY-trobe and getting no reaction. She wasn't interested in Arnold Palmer. She wasn't interested in the banana split. But then, wow, did she light up when I mentioned Mr. Rogers. LAY-trobe has something for everyone."

He says it may have started out as Lah-trobe, but it becomes LAY-trobe for every high school student on raucous Friday nights when the school cheerleaders begin to rev up the crowd. "All the cheers and school songs lead right to LAY-trobe. And that's what sticks."

He's right. Let's try it …

Gimme an L!

Gimme an A!

Now gimme a t-r-o-b-e!

What's it spell? Well, it doesn't spell "Lahhh" It spells "LAAA!" as in "Yay! or "Hooray!"

Pronunciations taught by ceaseless generations of choral teachers instructing how to vociferously sing the Latrobe alma mater reinforces it's LAY-trobe:

> *Oh, dear LAY-trobe High School to you*
> *We pledge to be loyal and true*

And while we're at work or at play
We'll honor and love Thee for aye.
Dear old LAY-trobe High!
Dear old LAY-trobe High!

Steve Kittey is editor of the Lah-trobe/LAY-trobe Bulletin. He comes down on the side of Lah-trobe. "Coming from a background that afforded me the opportunity to interact with many people from all walks of life, my unscientific research indicates 'Lah-trobe' is the more popular pronunciation, although both versions are acceptable."

Still, the Lah-trobeans argument has much support in the way of factual merits. If you dig a little deeper into the word roots you'll find grapevines. One source says the word has 17th century Germanic origins. This from surnamedb.com: "This rare surname is of aristocratic origin, and is recorded heraldically in Rietstap's "Armorial General" (circa 1680) as "de la Trobe" in Estonia. The name is believed to derive from the Middle High German "trube" (Old High German "t(h)ruba"), a bunch of grapes, and would be used of a vine-yard."

A bunch of grapes? I say this with affection, but my money would have been on a bunch of nuts.

Aristocratic origins is a surprise. Besides Arnold Palmer, the most aristocratic figure from around here is a puppet who answers to the name King Friday XIIIth. Royalty would seem to weigh in favor of the regal "Lah," instead of the guttural, "LAY," with its sexy implications.

A site devoting itself to proper pronunciations seemed promising, but in typical internet fashion what seemed to bestow resolution only compounded confusion. It offers for this two-syllable word a whopping 74 pronunciations.

It gets worse. It's not a definitive list. It's YouGlish, a YouTube-like site that shows 74 different speakers saying the word Latrobe in various speeches. A music historian mentions it in regards to town namesake Benjamin "Lah-trobe" and some sketches the architect made of banjos while visiting New Orleans. So evidence suggests Latrobe the man was as well-rounded as his namesake town was destined to become.

I enjoyed hearing one woman with a beguiling Australian accent talk about the challenging work environment in the "Lah-trobe" Valley. She said automation was taking away jobs, but she optimistically said whole new industries involving creative solutions could replace them. "For instance," she said, "the 'Lah-trobe' Valley is magnificent and would make a wonderful place for a tourist wine trail."

Now, that's my kind of problem-solver. I wonder if she knows Latrobe origins involve bunches of grapes or if she's just prone to giddy bursts of spiritual serendipity.

The Australian City of Latrobe has a population of 73,257 and is located in the Gippsland region of Victoria. Indeed, the website makes it seem like a very scenic place to go for a guzzle. I emailed the city manager to ask how they pronounced Latrobe, if there's anyone as famous as Palmer or Rogers from there and if they feel any kinship with us here in Westmoreland County. I didn't hear back, which I found rude.

Their loss. I was going to mail them a banana split.

The city is not the only institutional Latrobe in the antipodes. La Trobe University is in the Melbourne suburb of Bundoora. The University is named after Charles Joseph La Trobe (1801-1875), the first governor of Victoria.

So the name, while not common, does enjoy a proud and fertile global reach.

I sought answers from the browse-worthy HowManyOfMe.com website (tagline: *"There are 329,463,944 people in the U.S. How many have your name?"*

As always before getting down to business, I let my mind enjoy a pointless ramble.

The results: In the U.S. right now, there are three Christopher Rodells; 66 Arnold Palmers; 453 Fred Rogerses; and for the umpteenth year in a row zero Hap Hazards, which was the name I used on my first fake ID.

And there's not a single Benjamin Latrobe alive in the land. But of the 122 Latrobes in America, and I lucked into talking to one who was a blood relation of our town namesake. He's Charles "Rusty" Latrobe of Monkton, Maryland, a popular real estate agent for 40 years. He's the great-great-great-great-grandson of Benjamin Latrobe. And the two have more than chromosomal DNA in common.

Turns out neither Latrobe has ever set foot in Latrobe.

"But, I'm a big Arnold Palmer fan. He's the greatest."

Okay, then for our purposes he qualifies as an expert witness. So is it Latrobe or is it Latrobe?

"It's Latrobe. It's always been Latrobe."

He pronounced it … Lah-trobe!

So I — and so many others — have been flat wrong all these years. Lah-trobe does sound French. And like the French have on occasion done throughout history, I surrender. I was wrong.

The grit is gone. The sophisticates have won.

Lah-trobe is a French-sounding place after all.

Well, Lah-Dee-Dah.

Or is it LAY-Dee-Day?

Chapter 12

Good Deeds

I recently asked a friend if she knew of anyone who did any Fred Rogers-worthy good deeds or random acts of kindness right here in Mister Rogers' Neighborhood. She thought about it and said no. She couldn't think of a single one.

It's an instance of recollection being eclipsed by familiarity. She's been witness to multiple good deeds being done by her boyfriend, Larry. Nearly every time he sees me at Flappers he tells bartenders Zach or Aaron to buy me a double shot of Wild Turkey on the rocks

We exist in a time of such colossal interpersonal and social media hostility, we've become blinded to all the tiny kindnesses that float around in our fragile ecosystems.

And I'm not kidding. I do consider Larry buying me hootch to be an authentic good deed. Sure, it's not like he's offering me a vital organ for life-saving transplant — and if he keeps buying me drinks we may put that sort of generosity to the test — but it's a wonderful gesture that can have a positive ripple effect on the whole bar.

It'll improve my mood when it's flagging. It'll save me disposable income, which I might shower on a sad-looking stranger. Or who knows? I might reciprocate and buy Larry one back. We might spend the rest of the evening arm 'n' arm singing old ABBA songs before we settle in to start crying about our daddies. Because you just never know.

My point is we have no idea how even the most minuscule gesture — holding a door, making friendly and reassuring eye contact with a sidewalk stranger — might resonate with the recipient.

Mental health studies on altruism indicate doing good deeds reduces stress, improves emotional well-being and even improves physical health. One study found that adults over 50 who volunteered about four hours a week were 40 percent less likely than non-volunteers to have developed hypertension four years later.

So do as much or as little as you can — even if it's just buying a buddy a drink.

Or as Fred says, "The real issue in life is not how many blessings we have, but what we do with our blessings. Some people have many blessings and hoard them. Some have few and give everything away."

I'm like most of you in that I'm rarely in a position to do a high-profile good deed. But there is an alternative to doing one superheroic, headline grabbing good deeds.

Just do a bunch of low-profile ones.

Life Lesson on ...

Waking Up Determined to do Good

It was more a wish than a prayer, more an expression of dissatisfaction that I was unable to have more of an impact on humanity. But in July 2017, I distinctly remember waking up and thinking, gee, I wish I was in position to do more good deeds.

That's the kind of thinking I do on my daily strolls around the neighborhood. I'm not talking about saving cats from trees or diving in front of a bullet intended for an unworthy target. I don't have an urge to don a cape and save the world. But I thought it would be nice to help some little old lady cross the street so she'll know the world isn't as scary as the headlines all hint.

Lo and behold, not a half mile into my walk the opportunity to do a true good deed nearly fell in my lap.

It wasn't a little old lady. It was a big middle-aged one. My description will sound contrived but I swear it is factual.

She was what Dr. Hannibal Lechter described as "roomy." That was his euphemism for a woman of large proportions. She had stringy hair, was sweating profusely and, as I was about to discover, she had no front teeth.

It may be unkind, but my first impression was that from behind she resembled a pack mule, an observation based on her appearance and her apparent mission. She was carrying six plastic bags strained full with groceries -- three bags in each hand -- and a surf-board sized raft of generic toilet paper. She and I were both walking in the same direction on this humid, 85-degree day. I was gaining on her fast. She set down one armload of bags to adjust and catch her breath.

Now, understand, I didn't specify in my wish that the recipient of my good deed resemble a movie star. That didn't enter my thoughts. So if this was a test, I passed with flying colors.

"You look like you could use a hand," I said.

She smiled, a little embarrassed, that toothless smile scary enough to make an orange jack-o-lantern green with envy.

"Oh, no, I'm fine," she said.

Nonsense, said I. I'm out for a walk. Please let me assist.

It didn't take too much convincing for Donna to agree. I told her I was happy to help. With sweat drops rolling down both of our noses, we proceeded. She had about a mile to go, she said. No, she didn't own a car. She walked about once every two weeks to the grocery store and lugged it all back to her Main Street home.

She was very pleasant and grateful, but I was struck by how much awkward silence is involved in a mile-long walk with a perfect stranger.

She'd certainly seen enough TV to know that lots of no-good trouble can come from walking home with a stranger. And, me, I'd read enough Penthouse Forum letters to know that interesting things can happen when meeting a stranger.

She may have wondered if I was a psychopath (I'm not, at least, not yet). She may have wondered if I was going to ask for money or sex. I wondered if she was going to offer me some sex. It wasn't easy work and may have been worth a little sex. The bags were imposing.

"You're making me carry the heavy ones, aren't you?" I joked.

If she was nervous about me, she gave no hint of it. She smiled pleasantly almost the whole way. I think she was really grateful I came along when I did.

I was glad, too. I wonder if Donna would have gotten into my car if I'd have pulled over to offer her a ride. Probably not. I doubt I would.

During one of our block-long silences I started hoping my friends and people from church would drive by and recognize me. The sight of me walking and carrying the groceries of a strange, large woman armed with enough toilet paper to weather a nuclear winter would have made for a great scandal, one I'd have been happy to encourage. We did look like a couple, I'm sure. She was smiling because someone had stopped by to ease her burden on a miserable day.

I was smiling because my spontaneous urge to do a good deed had been fulfilled. It gave me a soulful sort of happiness to have by chance been in a position to help someone who really needed it.

I got to her door, set the groceries down, said I was glad to have been able to help and enjoyed meeting her.

She smiled a big, toothless grin and spared us both any additional awkwardness by just saying thanks rather than inviting me in for a topless massage.

So just doing the good deed would be all I'd get to feel good and felt good enough.

Sort of like some sex for the soul.

Life Lesson on ...

Good Deeds at the Dry Cleaner

Okay, first let me tell you about my good, altruistic deed and then I'll tell you the reasons why you shouldn't follow suit. And usage of the word "suit" is apt.

That's what I was there at the dry cleaners to pick up. It was a seasonal sort of summer suit, so I'd been leisurely about picking it up at the local dry cleaners. To clarify: the suit isn't leisure; I am. Had I picked the suit up a month previous when it was ready, the instigating transaction may never have occurred. But it did.

Here's what happened:

I walked into the local dry cleaner ready for friendly service. The ladies there are sweet as Delta tea and just as sunny. But the friendly smiles weren't what caught my eye. What did was something I prefer to avoid during my daily routine.

It was the black and gray uniform of the Pennsylvania State Police. It was hanging there in prominence smack dab in front of the five rows of -- who knows? -- perhaps a thousand items of bagged and dry-cleaned cloths.

I'm ashamed to admit it, but my first instinct when seeing that vacant suit was, "Run!"

Can't help it. It's in-bred. I have friends who are state policemen and I've enjoyed golfing with them. But the uniform itself usually means a day-ruining event. That's why I was surprised by the impulse I felt seizing me.

"How much is the bill for that officer's uniform?"

The old lady looked perplexed. She turned and looked through bifocals at the pink receipt. It was $24.73.

"Let me have that one, too," I said. "I'd like to pay for it."

Like many of you, I was deep into tough times. Income's near zero. If I donate right now, it's going to go to the Salvation Army, not the guy who's going to bust me with a $135 citation for going 42 in a 35-mph zone.

But here in western Pennsylvania there'd been a heartbreaking rash of officer shootings. So I paid for the officer's dry cleaning and the sweet dry cleaning lady was overwhelmed. "Well, how kind of you!" she gushed. "What's your name and phone number? I want to pass this along. I'm sure the officer will want to thank you."

I declined. "Just tell him thanks for all he does for us."

And I practically danced out of the shop. I felt great. I'd done an impulsive good deed for a worthy stranger and didn't taint it by seeking credit.

So why am I tainting it now? As a warning because of what's been happening to me ever since. See, I walked out of that dry cleaning shop not only feeling good, but also, yes, convinced something good was now likely to happen to me. We all like to believe in karma. We who consider ourselves good like to believe that our good deeds will eventually resonate and be rewarded. Sooner the better.

I felt so good that I thought I'd try generate some web campaign to get dry cleaning customers to anonymously pay for bills for uniformed police and armed forces. Certainly, among the hundreds of clothes being dry cleaned at any given moment, there are some uniforms worn by brave citizens who put their lives on the line for us.

It's such a simple gesture and is a great way to say thanks.

Now, here's what happened in the hour after my good, anonymous deed:

- Got an IRS bill for $437 in penalties for a tax dispute that was resolved in the tax bureau's favor.
- My six-month-old computer malfunctioned. I drove 90 minutes to Pittsburgh three times in the following seven days to get warranty service. Lost about two days of data and felt rash-inducing anxieties all week.

- Heard little sawing noises in the attic above the bed. Went up to investigate and found puddles of water on the plastic insulation. The snow-covered roof's leaking and needs replacing. Our baffled bug and critter guy couldn't discern what's making the noises. The disconcerting sawing noises continue unabated and I lay there sleepless each night awaiting a nest of mice to break through the ceiling and fall on my face.
- The snows that have since topped a total of 52 inches began to fall and continue to do so. I'm beginning to feel like Jack Torrance in "The Shining."
- Learned the kid needs braces.

So given how cockeyed karma's reacted to my good deed, will I ever voluntarily pay for another officer's dry cleaning?

Oh, absolutely.

Life Lesson on ...

WWJD about Latrobe's Homeless Dude (and What I Did)

I was succumbing to a morning need for fuel when my conscience was confronted with a WWJD moment.

These happen to me all the time, mostly in places where the risen Christ wouldn't be caught dead, places like the drive-thru lane at the Route 30 McDonald's.

Now, I know better than that. I know McDonald's is unhealthy, its entire corporate premise is environmentally belligerent, and it owes its colossal origins to Ray Kroc, one of America's most despicable scoundrels (I highly recommend the '17 Michael Keaton flick "The Founder").

WWJD?

He'd breakfast at The Youngstown Grille!

Locally-owned, friendly, affordable, generous portions and it's all delicious.

Jesus hasn't been there (yet!) but Arnold Palmer used to go there all the time for French toast. So if you can't get a Yelp! review from The King of Kings getting a posthumous one from The King will have to do.

But on some days I just need fuel and that means fast food. I get a Sausage Biscuit w/ cheese and a small Coke for $2.32. How they do it for so little is a wonder. I donate the 68-cent change to Ronald McDonald House because it's what I believe Jesus would do.

So I pull in and that's when I see Latrobe's homeless man. I'm sure there are many more and having even one is a defeat for a community I'm proud to call home. But this gent is our most visible one.

He pushes a Giant Eagle grocery cart that contains what I assume are all his earthly belongings. He looks maybe 50, but who knows? Elements of this harsh winter may have prematurely aged him.

I don't know what Jesus would do, but here's what I did:

In addition to my usual order I had them throw in an Egg McMuffin that set me back another $2.79 for a total of $5.11 (the Golden Arches charity scored another 21 cents so I was feeling pretty good about my pious altruisms).

So I clear the second window and see the guy is on the move. He's pushing his cart toward Rt. 30.

I roll down my passenger side window and shout, "Hey, man, I have something for you!"

He turns to look then coldly ignores me. His rudeness has me wondering if he's a former literary agent. That's a common literary agent's reaction to my offers. He continues pushing the cart toward the highway crossing.

And the chase is on!

I'm stuck at the red light watching him hump it up the hill on the driveway between Sharky's and the Walgreens. I pass him and pull into Walgreens parking lot. I park the car and get out with that steaming 410-calorie gut buster in my hand.

He sees me again and keeps on going. It's like I'm dealing with a nervous cat.

"Hey, I thought you might like an Egg McMuffin," I say. "It's still hot. Should hit the spot."

Nothing. He keeps on going.

Me, I surrender. I did what I thought was my best and I could not break through. He was unwilling to accept my charity. I get back in my car and drive away and as I do, I give him one last look. What I see surprises.

He's beaming at me. Honest, he's grinning like I would if he'd just handed me a McDonald's sack stuffed with $100 bills.

It's very odd. I spend most of the morning confused by the entire episode.

What would Jesus do?

I like to think He'd persuade the man to get in his 2007 Saturn Vue with 210,000 miles on it and drive him home where He'd nurture him to soulful health. I'm tempted to do that very thing. If it works out, it would be the best thing I'd do in my entire life.

But Jesus, a lifelong bachelor, never had to ask Himself WWVD? I do.

What would Val or any spouse do if I showed up with a disheveled stranger and told her to clear a spot on the couch? She barely tolerates the hours I spend with drinking buddies who have somewhere to go when the bartender yells last call.

So I ended up tossing the Egg McMuffin in the trash and left Latrobe's most visible homeless man to fend for himself, and me wondering if my good intentions will make a positive difference in my Judgment Day fate.

I hate to see the sandwich go to waste, but I'm one of those guys who worries about saving his figure while simultaneously still saving his soul.

Chapter 13

Married by Mr. Rogers

The I.R.S. reports in 2018 that 84,000 men — and women — listed their occupation as "Elvis impersonator." They perform in clubs, at parties, and fulfill every role a festive America might need. It's a phenomenon that transcends both borders and genders. Australia, for instance, has a performer that bills herself as the only Down Under female Elvis impersonator. "Ladies and gentleman, please give a warm Sydney welcome for …

"ShElvis!"

Elvis, of course, is revered for his charisma, his musicianship, his message and for his legacy of universal kindness that inspires still.

Any of that sound vaguely familiar?

So there are enough professional Elvis impersonators, or "tribute artists," to fill a colosseum (how many ever-lovin' part-timers must there be?) yet it's impossible to find anyone, anywhere who'll impersonate or pay tribute to Mr. Rogers.

I know, the mere suggestion must leave you all shook up.

How about a Mr. Rogers one-man play starring, say, Bryan Cranston? I suggest Cranston because I remember one stellar "Breaking Bad" review that declared his Walter White was so evil he "made Tony Soprano look like Mr. Rogers."

People through the years have lined up on Broadway to see

one-man plays about Albert Einstein, Lyndon Johnson, Nelson Mandela, Eleanor Roosevelt and all manner of famous and infamous.

Who wouldn't want to spend 90-minutes in the Land of Make-Believe hearing "Fred" talk about his life lessons and how they apply to today's tumultuous news events. Just having him read his greatest wisdom hits aloud would be eminently fulfilling.

It worked for Bruce Springsteen. His "Springsteen on Broadway" made $2.5 millon a week over a 58-week run at the Walter Kerr Theatre. A "Mister Rogers on Broadway" could make more than that.

It could make a difference.

Because it's becoming clear, Fred appeals to every demographic. Kids, sure, but his message is one most adults yearn to hear — even adults whom you'd think would be calloused to pretty phrasings about things like love, kindness and sharing. Men like blue-collar working man Pat Gianella. He lives in the Mount Washington section of Pittsburgh that overlooks the Golden Triangle. He can practically hear the cheers from Heinz Field when the Steelers score.

You'd think a guy like Gianella would start his day watching sports, news or political bickering.

Wrong!

"I start everyday with 'Daniel Striped Tiger,'" he says. "It soothes me and puts me in the right frame of mind."

And it goes without saying, but proper framing is essential for any successful carpenter.

You can tell he's a humble man because it takes him about five minutes of prodding about his career accomplishments before he finally gets to the detail most of us would blurt out moments after saying howdy.

"My wife and I were married by Fred Rogers," says Gianella of their 1983 wedding.

It's fitting to return to the Elvis analogy. Elvis impersonators have married tens of thousands of couples in Las Vegas alone. But Elvis himself never presided over anyone's wedding.

Fred Rogers was an ordained Presbyterian minister; in his lifetime, this man known for all the values that sanctify any successful marriage, presided over just three. It's a pity he didn't do more. He had a gift.

Ask Patsy's bride, Cathy Tigano Gianella. "Oh, I was a wreck," she says. "I was panicking. It all just seemed so crazy. I was in my slip and I heard this knock on the door and it was Fred. I said, 'Fred, I'm scared to death!'

"And he immediately began calming me by saying, 'Cathy, there's a lot of love out there. I can just feel it. We all want it to happen and you're going to be just fine. You met in the Land of Make-Believe, now let's make this real.'

"His mere presence was so calming. Truly, he was a modern-day Jesus Christ."

Have you ever had a boss worthy of that comparison? An uncle? A pastor?

And he was, indeed, their boss. Cathy was a WQED set designer, Patsy a station stage hand. So Fred wasn't being metaphorical. They did meet on the set of the Land of Make-Believe. The pair were friends first, good friends, for five years, before it dawned on them that a couple who worked so well together, so joyfully, really ought to give true romantic togetherness a real shot.

One year later and Patsy was pestering her to wed. But she'd been married before and it hadn't worked out. She was leery of going through another big Catholic wedding so she blurted out she'd marry him, but only if he could get Fred to perform the ceremony.

And up the stairs they went.

Delighted, he said, yes, but said it had to be done on Saturday, just days away. He'd be shooting a "Tonight Show" guest spot and then it was off to Nantucket for the summer.

Could they do it?

Yes!

"I remember walking out of that office and seeing Margy Whitmer (producer)," Cathy said. "She was always in control and knew everything that was going on. She asked what just happened in Fred's office. I said, 'Fred just agreed to marry us on Saturday!' Her mouth just flew open. She said, 'Do you know he gets hundreds of requests to perform wedding ceremonies each year and he turns them all down?'"

It was different with Patsy and Cathy. They were like family, and different still in their sweet dispositions. "He was always telling Patsy how nice I was."

Imagine being called nice by Fred Rogers. It'd be too negative an analogy to say it's a case of the pot calling the kettle black. More like the sugar calling the syrup sweet.

Up to that point it had seemed, as preposterous as it sounds in hindsight, that it was just like a friend doing them a favor. It's important to understand how they knew Fred, not as a celebrity, but as a benevolent boss who just happened to be an ordained minister. So they didn't expect any fanfare for a backyard wedding in a crowded ethnic neighborhood on a sweltering July day. Remember, too: no social media. Those quaint notions detonated when they turned the corner on Augusta Street.

"Never, never did I realize just how big he was until that day," she says. "We drove up and there were hundreds and hundreds of people lining the streets. There were people on rooftops. Kids in trees or on parents' shoulders. Everyone waiting to see Fred."

Without having done anything regal, Patsy and Cathy had become the hometown version of Prince Charles and Lady Di.

What she'll remember most was basking in the serenity of a man imbued with so much grace and kindness.

"He just brought so much peace to everything he did," she says. "As he was talking to me, he started fixing my hair. He was just so soothing. I can't think of anyone who wasn't affected by just being in his presence. Oh, how I wish he was alive today, just to be there for all the children."

Imagine the pressure of being that good, that inspirational, of never falling short of the incredibly high mark the world sets for you and you've imposed on yourself. Then imagine somehow surpassing it by being scrupulous about remembering the little things so many of us so casually overlook because they're, well, just the little things.

"Yeah, every year on July 2nd, we'd get an anniversary card with a sweet little note from Fred," Cathy says. "Every year."

You don't have to be the guy who saves the world if you can at least be the guy who remembers to send the thoughtful greeting cards to the folks who do. Because the little things add up.

Maybe I have it all wrong. Maybe the world is full of Mr. Rogers impersonators.

We pay tribute to him every time we're kind to one another.

Chapter 14

When You're in no Mood to See People & You See Fred Rogers

Did you ever have one of those days when nothing was going right? You were angry, in pain, feeling put upon, your future was filled with doctor-prescribed torment. Steve Kalinsky, then 27, was having that very day back in 1995. He was suffering from temporomandibular joint disorder, a painful jaw condition that back then was treated with strong painkillers and vigorous, invasive massage that seemed to surpass the initial pain in demonic throbbing.

And, oh, yeah, to endure the therapeutic treatments he had to on a miserable day drive to and locate parking in a part of Pittsburgh notorious for traffic chaos. As he describes it, he was operating amidst a "tsunami of anger, pain, despair and hopelessness." And that very last thing he wanted was contact with another human being who might offer a sunny alternative to his doom-filled day. He wanted none of those awkward human encounters where you might have to hold the door for a stranger, express civil gratitude or acknowledge that, gee, maybe the world wasn't such a grim place after all.

In short, he says, "I was the world's angriest and most unhappy man and the last person you want to see when you're feeling like that is the world's kindest man. But that was my fate. I ended up bumping into Fred Rogers."

Bumping into him like four times. The pair parked simultaneously down the street from the chiropractor's office where neither of them knew they both had concurrent appointments. Steve noticed the trim older gent walking slightly slower in front of him. Impatient, but not wanting to rudely just barrel past him, he allowed the stranger to make his way to the door first.

"We're practically shoulder-to-shoulder as we get to the door," he said. The proximity led to a civility mano-a-mano between the pedestrians, one of those endless pantomime, you first, no, please, after you. The thing that made this one so memorably different was it involved the self-described World's Angriest Man — and the other who turned out to be — Fred Rogers.

"He was fumbling with an umbrella and I figured the polite thing to do was to open and hold the door for him." Without making any eye contact, he heard a comforting voice say, "Thank you!"

"I look up and right there, larger-than-life, was Mister Rogers. The first thing he noticed was he's much taller than you'd think, he said. That's true. Rogers was 6 feet tall and people often expressed surprise at his size.

"Now, I wasn't in the mood for any chit chat, but how do you snub a smiling Fred Rogers?"

You don't. Still frowning, he said, "You're welcome."

Understand, too, that Kalinsky is a long-time entertainment photographer. He is immune to being starstruck. Yet there was just something compelling about being around a man world-famous for civility and kindness and seeing him firsthand behaving with such kind civility.

Kalinsky was about to get a lesson in the art of being defiantly kind, a practice perfected by Rogers where someone is so thoughtful, cheerful, hopeful, encouraging, good and genuinely nice — so positively human — that "normal" people think you're just plain weird.

Once inside, they mounted the steps — this time with Fred motioning Kalinsky to lead — by now sensing they were destined to wind up taking turns sitting on one another's lap in the same waiting room. By the time they'd waltzed into the waiting room it was again Kalinsky's turn to allow Fred to go first.

"By now, I was mellowing a bit at the absurdity of me and my mood trying to maintain my surliness in the face of his relentless kindness, I guess you could call it, and it was my turn to wave him ahead. Plus, I was really curious to see his signature on the sign-in sheet."

It's distinctive with theatric swoops on the capitalized letters as if the "F" and the "R" were taut sails affixed to mizzen masts being filled by surface gusts. "It could be a font of its very own," he says.

They both settled in to fulfill the primary obligation of those consigned to waiting rooms: They waited. But not before Rogers did two things that led Kalinsky to recall another iconic entry.

"Just like I remember him doing on his show, he took off his coat and carefully put it on a hanger. Then he sat down and just like he did on TV, he carefully removed his footware. Only this time they weren't dress shoes, they were galoshes. And this was the point where I started looking around for a hidden camera. I thought I was the unwitting victim of some elaborate prank."

Kalinsky wonders if Rogers was in a particularly playful mood that day, maybe sensing his fellow visitor was in distress and in need of comic relief. Because as they both perused their periodicals they would look up and their eyes would momentarily meet.

"We're the only two in the waiting room and every time our eyes would lock, even for a split second, he'd say, 'Hello!' Happened, I think, three times."

Then the receptionist said, "Mr. Rogers!" and it was over. Rogers rose and with a smile and an affirming nod and it was off he went. Behind he left Kalinsky, not cheerful exactly, but at least bemused, hopeful, no longer angry.

"If it'd been a stranger, I don't know how I would have taken it," he says. "It would have seemed a little weird. But because it was who it was, it seemed perfectly normal. And that's really too bad. You can't get away with being extravagantly kind unless you're friends."

Yeah, that is too bad. What may be worse is how common and acceptable is for anyone — anyone — to go extravagantly unkind.

Kalinsky wonders were the conversation might have gone had Fred followed up even one of those "Hellos!" with, "And how are you doing today?"

Would he have confessed to having succumbed to the day's dark clouds, both internal and external? Would he have asked Fred how he does it? Would he have asked him how he remains so serenely chipper when the whole world is a "tsunami of anger, pain, despair and hopelessness?"

All he knows is this: "I'm living proof it's impossible to be angry about after talking to Fred Rogers."

Score one for defiant kindness.

Life Lesson on ...

Making Bad Days Better

I was in a lousy mood one Sunday a few years back. I'd allowed the holy blessing of dealing with my mother's dementia to feel momentarily burdensome, I was fatigued by persistent professional failings and, yeah, I'd once again lost the stupid lawn-mowing challenge (me and Paul have for years had a gentleman's bet over who could go the longest without being nagged, harassed, badgered or threatened into cutting the grass).

So I was in a bad mood.

Then it got worse.

What happened?

My then-16-year-old daughter asked, "So why are you in such a bad mood?"

The nerve. Of course, her keen insight made me seethe and demolished what little chance there was of a happy family night. I sulked. Slammed doors. Felt sorry for myself and generally behaved like adults stereotypically expect 16-year-old girls to behave.

I spent a lot of time wondering why her accurate diagnosis lit my fuse.

She wasn't being rude, but asking someone if they're in a bad mood is a sure way to put anyone in a bad mood. Really, she should have offered a soulful solution — and that we sometimes expect more from our children than we expect from ourselves is a topic for another day.

"What you need to do next time you sense I'm in a bad mood," I said, "is offer an incentive to brighten my mood. Say, 'You seem like you're having a bad day. Is there anything I can do to cheer you up?'"

There are thousands of ways a dear daughter can do this for a father or you can do it for a grumpy friend.

She could have said I look like I've lost weight, slept well and that my growing concerns about the need for hair plugs were unfounded. She could have said things were bound to get better, it was a nice day to golf or that next year I'd certainly win the annual no-mow lawn contest.

Any positive — even fibs — surpasses any negative.

My wife is actually very good at this without, I think, even being aware of it.

She knows when I'm acting like a jerk, but never stoops to the gracelessness of saying, "Hey, jerk! You're harshing everyone's buzz. Snap out of it!"

I'll never forget the time we had a huge blow up about something I've long since forgotten. But I do recall one memorable fact: I was leaving for work.

Yes, it was one of the eight days in 2014 when I'd been summoned to tend bar at old The Pond. So there are elements to this story akin to observing a solar eclipse from the back of an albino unicorn.

My Saturday shift had yet to begin and I was having a drink at the bar, understanding as I did the necessity of being liquored up before I began liquoring up friends and strangers.

When I saw her come through the door I tensed believing she was eager to resume hostilities in public.

That was not her intention. She smiled, sat next to me and asked Dave for a Yuengling. Her smile conveyed everything was going to be all right and in an instant reminded me why I fell in love with her in the first place.

She took a sad song and made it better.

We could learn a lot from Val.

These are contentious times. It's easy to get down, to let the news sour your disposition, to fall into a mood so bad it practically gives off a stink.

You know someone who right now is in a bad mood and you have the power to do something positive about it.

What are you waiting for?

Changing the world is a daunting task. Start by just changing one mood.

Thank you for reading. I must say, you look wonderful. Have you lost weight?

Chapter 15

Latrobe: A Land of Legends

Joe Comm is a Greater Latrobe elementary school teacher and the author of "Legendary Locals of Latrobe" (Arcadia Publishing, 2015). It stands out to me from other similar books about other towns in that it's thick and most of the mentioned locals are truly legendary.

"Latrobe is a special place known for its close neighborhood feel and the quality of its people, its intriguing characters and its everyday citizens who have made Latrobe's history legendary," Comm wrote.

You know about Fred Rogers and Arnold Palmer, the Steelers at Saint Vincent, Rolling Rock beer and the first banana split. Comm's 128-page book shares their impact and goes into detail about dozens of other legends. Our legendary firsts include: first all-professional football team; first non-stop airmail pickup; first Benedictine monastery.

Spoiler alert: I'm on p. 64! I made the cut, I guess, for my blog and for my '13 "Use All The Crayons!" book which enjoyed a promotional foreword and cover endorsement by true Latrobe legend Arnold Palmer. I was flattered to be included and pleased they used one of my favorite profile pictures, one of me peeking through a wreath of crayons, a cherished Father's Day gift. Either way, it's been a personal and professional boon for me to have hometown access to so many true legends. Here are some relevant updates on a few of our prominent legends.

Legend I:

So what was Arnold Palmer Really Like?

"What's Arnold Palmer really like?"

We used to get that question all the time and we could all give honest and informed answers. Prior to his September 25, 2016, death the answer was, "He's unavoidable." We'd see Palmer at the bars, the barber, the restaurants, the golf courses and sometimes at the grocery store bumming money.

My friend Joe Holliday told me how one time he was walking into the local Giant Eagle when he saw Palmer and a friend near the lottery ticket counter. Joe went up and introduced himself. It being a small town, Palmer got his dog, Mulligan, groomed at Holliday's girlfriend's doggie salon. After the initial chit chat, Palmer mistakenly assumed Holliday was there to play the lottery.

"He said, 'Give me $20, we'll split what we win.' Now, I can't say no. I reach into my wallet and all I had was $20. So I fork over my last $20 to Arnold Palmer who at the time was worth about $700 million."

They bought four scratch-offs and took turns. And they didn't win squat.

Palmer shrugged and magnanimously said, "Well, you win some, you lose some."

Joe replied, "Well, you've won a helluva lot more than me!"

The question, "What's Arnold Palmer really like?" was common enough I was able to craft two handy answers: "What's Arnold Palmer really like? Arnold Palmer is perfectly cool, authentic and refreshing. If he were a drink he'd be an Arnold Palmer."

What's he like?

"If Arnold Palmer were the only member of The Greatest

Generation it would still be The Greatest Generation solely because it included Arnold Palmer."

He's often referred to as a legendary golfer. But describing Palmer as a legendary golfer was like describing Nelson Mandela as a successful parolee. It didn't begin to do justice to a momentous legacy.

He was an enthusiastic philanthropist bestowing countless millions on dozens of hospitals, scholarships and charitable organizations. He owned famous resort golf courses, car dealerships, golf equipment companies, golf apparel companies -- he even owned The Golf Channel. And he was the hip drink impresario behind the international sensation that is Arnold Palmer Teas.

Kirk Douglas said about him in 1970 that no one he'd ever met -- not Sinatra, John Wayne or Ronald Reagan -- had more charisma than Palmer.

I always felt his passing was like a tutorial to understanding Latrobe. There was, sure, the obligatory sadness that he'd died, but it quickly morphed into euphoria that he'd lived. It was one of the greatest lives of the last century and he generously shared so much of it with us.

That was a key difference between Fred Rogers and Arnold Palmer; shortly after graduating college, Fred relocated to Pittsburgh. He'd come back to visit, but it wasn't like we'd see him around town in all in the grocery store, the restaurants, the barber shop or the dozens of other places where Palmer seemed to visit on a daily basis. It's just that Fred was no longer present. Palmer was the exact opposite. Not only was Palmer present, he at times seemed downright hard to miss.

I thought of that the week after he'd died when I popped in for a drink at Flappers, the second-floor bar right here at the Tin Lizzy. I'd spent a great night with my friends and didn't feel like heading home just yet, so I pulled into the Tin parking lot — and talk about your reflexive vehicular maneuvers.

The bar was empty, but on the porch there were about a dozen people having what sounded like a riot every 90 seconds.

I asked the bartender what was going on.

"Oh, they're telling Arnold Palmer stories," she said. "They've been out there for two hours. I don't think they're ever going to leave."

I stayed for about 30 minutes and it was like you could have set your watch; a roar of laughter every 90 seconds. I thought someone was going to call the cops.

John Paul Newport of the *Wall Street Journal* wrote on Palmer's 80th birthday, "Lasting popularity of Palmer's magnitude simply cannot be explained."

Oh, yes it can. Let me give it a shot:

He was worth in the neighborhood of $800 million when he died. But he lived like every single one of us could live. He was kind, he had style, he was competitive without being bitter. He treated the guy who worked on his car the same way he treated the guy who worked on his heart.

He could have been pampered in palaces around the planet, but he never left home — and to his dying day, he bragged about the splendors of that home, ones often hidden to many of its lifelong inhabitants.

So, yes, Arnold Palmer the man was like Arnold Palmer the drink in that both were perfectly cool, authentic and refreshing. But there is one key difference. There will be plenty of one around, mass produced and long in demand.

But the original will never be duplicated.

It's too bad. He's gone for good.

Legend II:

The History of the 1st Banana Split & Bank Robbery Festival

Latrobe's first Great American Banana Split Festival in 2013 was a three-day extravaganza celebrating the official recognition that our old Tassel's Pharmacy was in 1904 the site of the creation of the world's first banana split by then 23-year-old pharmacist David Strickler. Highlights included a banana split-themed sock hop, a banana split-themed street festival, a banana split-themed song contest and a bank robbery.

Can you believe it?

I mean the bank robbery not being banana split themed.

Yes, as many of our city officials were attending to the downtown ceremony where the historical marker was being unveiled, a crafty robber seized on the inconvenient logistics and held up the Citizens Bank one mile away before racing away to, I'm guessing, the Great American Crystal Meth Festival.

Oh, how I wish I could report the culprit was apprehended after slipping on a bank parking lot banana peel.

He and his driver got away with an undetermined amount of cash, which is now, like the suspects themselves, covered in gaudy red security ink. Reports say the radio transmitter-controlled dye packs exploded.

The same thing happened to Gale and Evelle Snoats in "Raising Arizona." I can't believe any would-be bank robbers haven't seen it. It's a great movie. Very funny and parts of it are like vo-tech school for stupid crooks.

These exploding dye packs are very sound deterrents to criminal activity. They either stain or destroy the money, burn the robber with heat and tear gas elements and leave the getaway vehicles and the robbers themselves covered in indelible Disperse Red No. 9 ink.

Too bad they don't have an equivalent deterrent to the Wall Street bankers who use clever accounting tricks to rip off banks and taxpayers of untold millions.

Oh, wait. They do. It's . . . none!

I remember encouraging organizers to take extra precautions in succeeding years as Latrobe continues to celebrate its role in the creation of America's heirloom dessert.

For ceremonial purposes, I'd at least like to see if sponsor Dole Fruits will pay to fill the packs with Disperse Banana Yellow No. 9 ink.

Either way, I'm glad no one was hurt. I was in that very bank the previous week at the very time of the robbery. That's my mother's bank and I use that branch when I need to administer to her meager funds.

So, naturally, I spent a good deal of the weekend wondering how I'd have reacted had the crime happened before my eyes.

Would I have tried to be the hero? Not a chance.

I would have run.

After all, turning yellow and splitting is for at least one weekend a year in Latrobe the civic thing to do.

Legend III:

Stop Drinking Rolling Rock!
It's Made in New Jersey

He was a nice earnest young man, very polite and friendly. Exactly the kind of person no one should want to murder. But that was my instinct for reasons that will be clear to anyone who cares about things like truth and tradition.

He was drinking a Rolling Rock. Bragging about it.

We were making idle chatter at the Pour House, an outstanding Irish pub in Carnegie, birthplace of Pittsburgh Pirate great Honus Wagner, when he asked where I lived.

I told him Latrobe.

"Man, I've always wanted to go there and tour the brewery," he said. "Rolling Rock's the best. One day I want to come see where it's made."

"Then you'd better plug Newark into your GPS," I said, "because that's where they've been making it since 2006."

I really shouldn't have been mad at him. How was he to know?

Ever since 2006 when Anheuser-Busch bought the Rolling Rock brand, the beer producers have been successfully hoodwinking beer drinkers into thinking the beer was still made in the "glass-lined tanks of ol' Latrobe," a phrase that still appears on the charming green bottles.

It infuriates me.

See, I've loved Rolling Rock longer than I've loved my family. It's been there for me since I started drinking beer back in, I think, the 5th grade.

And unlike those in my family, Rolling Rock had never done anything to break my heart. Of course, my family's never done anything to give me a skull-pounding hangover so I guess it's a wash in regards to which entity's been more debilitating.

But I had a real fondness for Rolling Rock all my drinking life. I drank in college because we loved the taste and because the little 7-oz. pony bottles — we called 'em grenades — were the perfect size to heave empty at the trains that ran right through the Ohio University campus in Athens.

It's the beer they drank in the little western Pennsylvania neighborhood bars where they filmed "The Deer Hunter."

I drank it with apostolic pride when I lived in Nashville. Heck, we all did. I have pictures of my going away party where the tables were littered with empty horses.

The horse was the 12 ouncer; the ponies were 7. It all tied into the equine theme painted in white on the green bottles. When they came out with a dark beer in about 1996, my buddy started calling it "horse manure."

Everything about it was charming. It was small town. It had great mystique. It had that "33" on the label.

Some theorized that was the year a horse named Rolling Rock won the Kentucky Derby (false); others said it was because 1933 was the year Prohibition was repealed (true, but merely coincidental).

The real reason was because when the beer was first being bottled the owners put the iconic little "from the glass-lined tanks of ol' Latrobe" phrase on the backs of the mock-up. The saying was 33 words long (true) and they put that at the bottom — "33" — so the printer would know how much per-word to charge.

I remember telling that story in college at parties and then watching the trivia spread. I could tell it was spreading, too, because you could see all the lips moving as disbelievers began counting the words.

It was college, but none of the Bobcats had yet learned how to count in their heads without moving their lips.

Then in 1989, fate could no longer be denied and I moved to Latrobe.

Arnold Palmer! Fred Rogers! The first professional football game! Birthplace of the banana split!

And Rolling Rock!

I'd found me a home. I was one of two bureau reporters right in Latrobe, just down the street from Latrobe Brewing. It was right there. You could see it. You could smell it.

I remember one time back when I was still doing local reporting and was responsible for getting the daily hospital admittance reports at Latrobe Hospital.

I remember one fall morning walking out of the hospital with my lists and being greeted by this young family that was from out of town and unfamiliar with the local aroma. It smelled like cooking cereal.

"Yuck! What is that smell?" they asked.

As we were standing outside the hospital, I was tempted to say something like, "Oh, this is when they burn the amputated limbs and other medical wastes!" Instead, I told the truth.

"That's the brewery where they make Rolling Rock."

I'll never forget the beatific transformation of their faces. The smell went from noxious to marvelous. "Oh! You don't say!"

The brewery seized on the small town charm of its brand and sponsored The Rolling Rock Town Fair at the Westmoreland County Fairgrounds in the early 2000s. Performers included the Red Hot Chili Peppers, Outkast, Nickelback, Stone Temple Pilots and a bunch of other bands that held zero appeal for me.

But I went because it was all just so cool. It was a true town fair. They had games, rides, cow-milking contests, the works. People came from all over the country and it was very special.

Then in 2006 it all went to hell.

Budweiser bought the brand and moved it out to Newark. It was the last time I ever paid for a Budweiser product.

The brewery went idle and 70 of my buddies were out of work from jobs they'd expected would sustain them, as it had their fathers, through to retirement.

Some in Latrobe turned to prayer.

Me, I turned to Yuengling, a fine Pennsylvania beer brewed in Pottsville.

A series of owners came and went. Iron City, another iconic western Pennsylvania brand, was mismanaged out of business in Pittsburgh. They began making that in Latrobe.

And through it all the New Jersey producers of Rolling Rock kept up the charade that the beer was made in the town they'd turned their back on.

Check out the Rolling Rock website: It's still designed to mislead visitors into believing it's made right here.

Drives me nuts.

And I can't keep up with what is made here. The brewery is booming.

Besides Iron City, they also brew Stoney's and trendy Southampton brands Double White, IPA, Atbier, Pumpkin, and Imperial Porter. They also brew Duquesne, another heirloom Pittsburgh brand that's become my go-to draft of choice.

They're doing great, as is Four Seasons Brewery, a craft brewery that in 2013 began operating in Latrobe and is going gangbusters.

But I miss the days when the beer world made perfect sense, when Latrobe made Rolling Rock, when Pittsburgh made Iron City and Newark made embarrassing mistakes involving sensible city governance.

The utter absurdity of it all was hammered home the summer of 2013 when we were in the Outer Banks on vacation. Val made a beer run and called from the store to see what I wanted.

"They have Heineken, LaBatts, Red Stripe, Corona . . ."

"Oh, get the Red Stripe. I haven't had that since our cruise."

Hooray beer!

Remember those Red Stripe ads? You had this ya-mon Rastafarian extolling the joys of the Jamaican-brewed beer by shouting, "Hooray beer!" It reminds me of our Caribbean cruise and seemed perfect for vacation, a little island beer on our little island getaway.

It wasn't till she brought it home and I studied the label that I realized just how out of tilt the beer world's become.

My Jamaican beer is now brewed in, ya mon, Latrobe. It's true.

There are still days when I'd like to get my hands on a Rolling Rock pony bottle.

It's just that now I want to heave it at the train before any one else gets a chance to buy it and help perpetuate a fraud.

Legend IV:

Lambs, Latrobe & Dr. Lechter

As has been noted, Latrobe has been the site of serious crime involving actual criminals. But the Land of Make-Believe once played a small part in tracking down one of the worst monsters in cinematic history. And I had a role in it all.

Seriously.

My role might have grown into something more substantial, but I got cut. And I mean cut in the purely Hollywood way. The monster was Hannibal Lechter.

Even many locals tend to forget that Latrobe was in "Silence of the Lambs." The 1991 film is only the third picture in movie history to win all top five Oscar categories — Best picture/director/actor/actress/adapted screenplay — and went on to earn more than $275 million.

I was writing features and news for *The Tribune-Review* when someone connected with production called and asked me if I'd like to be an extra. He told me to bring a suitcase and dress like a successful businessman.

Me? Act like a successful businessman? It'd be the greatest acting triumph since Sir Lawrence Olivier played Hamlet.

They did about a dozen takes of me and about 10 other people walking through the local airport terminal with Foster marching behind me in the mix. I remember trying to appear grave. I guess I was even less of an actor than I was a businessman because when we went to see the premiere they'd cut my 5-second scene. How cruel.

In fact, my buddy Bill Kenly, long-time local tavern owner, joined me for the day and is in the film for about 2 seconds. He's one of the two police officers shown when the plane lands at the Latrobe airport.

For me, the most interesting part of the day was the opportunity to spy Jodie Foster -- already an Oscar winner for her role in the 1988 film, "The Accused" -- eat lunch. Back then what was still a little regional airport had an Italian restaurant, The Blue Angel, where the cast and crew gathered for noon victuals.

I doubt Mr. Rogers would have approved of the etiquette breach, but I didn't take my eyes off Foster. My observations revealed she's dainty, as you might expect. She ordered her salad dressing -- it was French -- on the side so she could control portion consumption.

And she doesn't like being interrupted when she eats.

This became apparent when the late restaurant owner, Jimmy Monzo, a bombastic Italian gent, came over and asked if he could have his picture taken with her. He was going to put it up on the wall that featured glossy photos of him alongside luminaries like Ronald Reagan, Frank Sinatra and Arnold Palmer.

She politely, but insistently with her fork hovering in mid-air told him no and that she wished to be left alone.

Why, the old man was outraged, livid. It was an enormous snub, a public rebuke to boot. He literally had to be dragged away from a table in his own restaurant sputtering his indignations.

Who, he kept asking, does she think she is?

Foster, the consummate pro, acted like he'd become invisible. Or maybe she wasn't acting and ignoring commoners — even uncommon commoners like Jimmy — just came naturally to her. She is a big deal, but so were Arnold Palmer and Fred Rogers, two men with sterling reputations for dealing with both kings and commoners. Of course, they weren't raised in Hollywood.

I'd see that old man every once in a while over the next few years before he died and I'd always ask, just to get him going, that same question over and over: Who does that Jodie Foster think she is?

It was unkind of me, sure, but I the sight of him stewing over an increasingly ancient slight always shattered the tedium of my then-daily news duties.

It wasn't until nearly three decades later that Val and I'd become surprise chums with a friendly husband and wife pair who made a quirky contribution to the movie that will endure for as long as the title is uttered.

John and Sukey Jamison supplied the lamb for "The Silence of the Lambs!" And while the title lambs make no noise, our friends, natural and engaging storytellers, are capable of telling the story. It's a good story, too. See, they were having trouble believing Jodie Foster was filming a horror movie in Latrobe that would require their lambs.

"They'd told us the film involved a serial killer who skinned human carcasses," he said. "It sounded preposterous. Sukey and I didn't know what to make of it."

You could say the lamb farmers were initially feeling, well, sheepish!

As they describe it in their 2018 book, "Coyotes in the Pasture & Wolves at the Door," they reveled in the experience. "She and the rest of the crew seemed to respect what we were doing even though our part was over in Warhol's famous fifteen minutes. Very classy."

John, himself an amateur actor, compared being up-close and personal on such a famous movie to a kid getting to play catch with Joe DiMaggio.

They're too humble to consider it, but maybe Foster, Demme and crew sensed or had heard that the Jamisons and their lambs are superstars revered in top kitchens around the globe. Anthony Bourdain said the whole farm-to-table movement began with the Jamisons who were stubborn in their belief that the soil and the blend of grasses unique to the Latrobe area would lead to the world's tastiest and most sought-after lamb meat.

The Hollywood people may have all been outstanding in their field, but John and Sukey were one up on them. They have an actual field. It's a kind of success that can truly be called grassroots.

Chapter 16

Politics

A sweet woman with a sunshine disposition is a recent arrival from Texas. She's upbeat, optimistic, chipper and encouraging — the perfect personality we'd all like for a neighbor. She gushed about how me how much she loves her new home.

"The schools are great, the temperatures pleasant and *everyone is just so nice!*"

I hated to have to burst her bubble, but I told her straight up: "If that's the way you feel, then you haven't *met* everyone."

Everyone is NOT nice. Some are intolerant. Some are mean. Some are crude. Some are bullies. Some can be, er, cruelly judgmental!

Or so I hear.

She'll find this out, sadly, when she declares, perhaps innocently perhaps vociferously, her political leanings. Is she red or is she blue? Does she support open borders or family separation? Or let's just cut to the chase: Would she rather see Trump happy or lavender-haired, rainbow-hearted U.S. Woman's Soccer captain Megan Rapinoe?

Just typing the divisive questions makes my head hurt.

Our insane political passions are poisoning even the otherwise idyllic relationships here in the neighborhood.

Latrobe has become another one of those places where parents warn their children about the perils of social media malevolence and then take to social media to engage in perilously malevolent behavior. They rant, they bully, they poison once-vital friendships.

Somewhere along the way Facebook, a community unifier, became Hatebook, a lawless realm where like-minded tribes go to beat the war drums. Every one is looking to fight.

A sweet girl I know — and she's a real babe — told me she was saddened the other day when out of the blue a friend blocked her over mild political commentary.

"I went to comment on something she'd written and I saw she'd blocked me," she said. "I wasn't going to say anything mean. I just wanted to point out there are two sides to every story, maybe start a dialogue. And she blocked me. I couldn't believe it. I thought we were friends."

Who was this reckless firebrand?

My wife!

Yes, we're so divided even the mild-mannered Lutheran church organist must be censored.

I feel bad that anyone would do anything to make my sweetheart glum, but admit to feeling a bit more chipper knowing the frowny face for once didn't have anything to do with her realization she's married to me so at least there's that.

I daily grow more and more nostalgic for the times when I didn't know your politics and you didn't know mine. Heck, I'm daily growing more and more nostalgic for stupid cat videos.

The routine vitriol she sees among her friends — and Val doesn't hang with the tattooed roller derby set —- is shocking. She says people who have to make nice at things like PTA meetings savage each other online.

We are witnessing the death of polite society. Heck, many of us are complicit in the murder.

I know people who want to kill one another over yard signs. We persist — both sides — to try and change the minds of the mindless when there are no minds left to change.

I used to worry about America surviving the next election. Now I worry if Americans will survive one another.

I wonder what Fred would do. Is there a right way to disagree over things that matter so much to so many?

I'm just overcoming a difficult rift with some old friends with whom I agree on every political litmus test but one: I'm incapable of hating people with whom I disagree. I choose not to demonize them. I will not shun them in public. I try and understand why they think the way they do, a gracious courtesy I wish they'd extend to me. I try and see the good in them even if it means I have to really squint. The sole exceptions to this silver-lining philosophy are people who hate. I'm aware of the inherent contradictions, but the only people I truly hate are people who truly hate. I refuse to tolerate the intolerant.

So I'm not going to ridicule the many Trump supporters with whom I disagree on matters of policy and presidential conduct. It's as impractical as it is impolite.

I don't see any point to insulting the people who worship where I worship, who fix the brakes on my car or who work within spittin' distance of my take-out food. Some like-minded friends want me to mock, despise, berate, detest and question their right to exist, let alone vote. They want me to hate neighbors like Frank and tell him he's an idiot for keeping that Trump sign in his yard.

Hate Frank? How could I? Frank's my friend. Frank fixes my car. We get along. We talk football. We're both Steeler fans.

What possible good would come from me telling Frank I think he's an idiot for supporting Donald Trump? What would happen if, say, I said, "Frank, you've always done a good job keeping my jalopy running and charged me a fair price. But I can't abide having a Trumpster work on my car so this is goodbye. We're finished. May the fleas of a thousand rabid monkeys nest in your crotch the day after all your arms mysteriously become too short to scratch there. Goodbye, Frank. And, oh, let's go Steelers!"

It would likely hurt Frank's feeling or cause him to hurt mine. Then I'd have to find another honest, affordable mechanic who's willing to let me quiz him about his feelings over excessive redactions in the Mueller Report.

The nation has been enfevered over politics for about three years. Hatred reigns as Type A combatants devote their time to committing large chunks of Sun Tzu's "The Art of War." It seems particularly acute here in Latrobe (Youngstown) where an enterprising Trump supporter painted an 2-story rental property in star-spangled red, white & blue and installed in the front yard a 30-foot Donald Trump full-color metal cut-out.

I swear, every single driver that passes by salutes it with either a thumb or the finger. During the 2016 election furor, thousands of Trump supporters from all over America stopped by to marvel. Major news organizations sent reporters here to profile Trump Town. Having done dozens of similar magazine profiles, I was always disappointed when the writers failed to highlight the obvious contradictions between Mr. Trump's behavior and Mr. Rogers' storied kindness.

One article quoted many of my Trump-loving friends here at The Tin Lizzy and included two pictures that drew scornful remarks in the lively reader comments section including this: "These photos above are exactly what I've always imagined for a Trump-supporting environment. So many racist hickabillies & elderly people."

I took exception to the prejudicial jibes for personal reasons.

I was in the picture! Yeah, the picture centered on me and owner Buck Pawloski sipping cocktails and watching an afternoon ballgame (I told my wife it was pure flukey coincidence I happened to be in the bar when the picture was snapped).

Now, regular readers know I'm not a racist hickabilly. Heck, I still need someone to explain to me just exactly what a hickabilly actually is. And, hey, I'm not all that elderly, not as long as you're comparing me to someone like Santa Claus.

I've had narrow-minded friends ask how I could spend so much happy Tin Lizzy time with people with whom I often vehemently disagree. I tell them if I confined my conversation to purely enlightened and sophisticated folk mine would be a very lonely existence and I'd have to stop talking even to myself.

I don't think many local Trump supporters are even aware of it, but Trump has been to Mister Rogers' Neighborhood at least twice prior to campaigning for president.

He's a big Arnold Palmer fan and flew his jet to the Arnold Palmer Regional Airport to golf with The King. I spoke with bartenders, waitresses, locker room attendants and various club members and to a person they were complimentary. They said he was respectful and engaging.

They said he was the kind of gentleman those of us who oppose him wish he'd be when he was negotiating things like the future of NATO with folks like Angela Merkel.

It's become a small sort of legend, one I've cunningly nurtured, that the last question I asked Arnold Palmer was if he believed there was golf in heaven.

Spoiler alert! He did.

"Oh, I think there will be a lot of golf in heaven," he said. "I'll bet Nelson and Hogan are up there having a match right now. I know a lot of guys who've been good golfers who are looking forward to resuming great matches with friends and family just like they did here on earth. I think the courses will be a lot like the ones here. But the hazards will include clouds that get in the way of approach shots."

In fact, that was the second-to-last question I'd ever ask him. The last question, the one I knew we'd never use but I wanted to know, went like this:

"Almost every home in our neighborhood has a 'Donald Trump for President' sign in their front yard. You're the only person in town who actually knows Donald Trump. When are we going to see your Trump sign?"

Still smiling, his eyes got big and he said in what I'm going to call mock terror, "Oh, no! That's never going to happen! No way!"

Read into that what you wish. Was he saying he'd never support Trump or that he didn't support political signs in his finely landscaped yard.

I laughed, said thank you and goodbye. There would be no follow-up. I wasn't going to badger him about what he meant, how he felt and maybe risk losing a friend. Either way, I doubt Arnold Palmer had been sitting on a fence just waiting for my enlightenment on how to vote. There were many majestic words you could use to describe him. Undecided was not among them.

He would be dead in 33 days. I never saw our friend again.

So those are my feelings, thoughts and beliefs on the most divisive issue of the day.

I have my opinions, but I choose not to hate those whose opinions are contrary to mine. And I have trouble understanding why many of the people who are opposed to building physical walls are more than happy to construct truly ugly mental ones between themselves and the neighbors they see every day.

Like I think Fred Rogers would counsel, I refuse to hate anyone for any reason (the illogical exception, again, being those who hate for no reason), and I will persevere cheerfully and serene in the heartfelt belief that we're going to make it through all this unseemly turbulence, scarred but perhaps wiser from the wounds. And I will try not to contribute to the unholy tumult.

As it so says in the Book of Proverbs 26:21, English Standard Version, "As charcoal to hot embers as wood to fire, so is a quarrelsome man to kindling strife"

Biblical grilling tips!

Or as Fred says, "There are three ways to ultimate success: The first way is to be kind. The second way is to be kind. The third way is to be kind."

And as I say, if you know more Sun Tzu quotes than ones by Fred Rogers then you're probably an, er, jerk.

Life Lesson on...

Being Undecided

If I have the guts to pull it off on Election Day 2020, I'm pretty sure you'll hear about it, which means I'm pretty sure you won't. It's too bad, too, because I imagine it would be a dandy practical joke.

Like all great practical jokes there's nothing practical about it. I'd do it because I think it'll be funny.

It'll involve hours of standing, pained expressions, flop sweat and torrents of relentless public ridicule.

As I'm already a married father, I've got most of that down pat.

See, 2020, like 2016, will likely be the "Year of the Undecided Voter."

Those of us with the ability to make up our minds -- and apparently that's 99 percent of us -- will have endured two years and $2 billion of obnoxious ads trying to persuade about 1 percent of the electorate to vote for this one or that one.

They say after all that, after the debates, the ballyhooed jobless reports and robo callers, they -- gee whiz -- just can't up their minds.

I want to be that guy.

Few people understand the news media better than I. That's not as boastful as it sounds.

Having worked for many of the most high-profile media organizations in the world (and having been rejected by the rest), I have a unique grasp on what the media are seeking today.

And did you notice I used the grammatically correct media "are" instead of the commonly incorrect media "is?"

Told yinz guys I knew my, er, stuff.

I know that the biggest story of that day, bigger than even who wins, will be the identity of the undecided voter. Why'd they vote for who they did?

Every news outlet will be camped outside of the polling places all day trying to find these electoral kingmakers.

And I have a plan to ensure national exposure, which I'd then use to obnoxiously promote my latest book. Interested in that kind of publicity? Here's what you do:

Walk into the voting booth . . .

And never leave.

Camp there. Stay all day. Make them call the police to throw you out.

The reason I probably won't do it is because I know all the people at my polling place, am shy about causing a scene, and fear my shenanigans would harm my shameless attempts to get anyone to buy my book.

It's a pity because for the past eight years our polling place down at the local elementary school has been perfect.

We used to have those proper booths with the levers that pulled the drape shut behind you. The privacy made me feel secure.

Now our voting booths are those little electronic stations that leave voters fully exposed. I spend my whole time glancing over my shoulder in fear that some angry Trumpster is going to see I'm voting the straight Democratic ticket and pound me over the head with his big bag of gold bars Sean Hannity advised him to buy.

But the visibility in this case lends itself perfectly to my scheme.

I'd walk in, nod hello, sign my name and be ushered to the voting station. It would be perfectly nondescript.

Then time would tick by. Ten minutes. Thirty minutes. An hour. Hundreds of other voters will come and go . . . and I'll still be standing there.

But I wouldn't be standing still there.

No, it would be performance art of the highest order. I'd pace in a little circle. I'd look pensive. I'd look thoughtful. I'd look more anguished than James Dean in the scene from "Rebel without a Cause" where he falls to pieces screaming, "You're tearing me apart!"

All of this will alarm the polling workers who would clearly see they're dealing with an undecided voter. They won't know what to do so they'll call their supervisors. The media will show up to broadcast live reports of the man inside who can't make up his mind.

"One official said this middle-aged man has spent six hours at his voting station," the reporter will say. "Sources say he spent a 30 minutes doing EENIE-MEENIE-MINIE-MO before bursting into tears. He remains truly undecided."

I'd be seen praying for guidance and asking aloud questions to both candidates like they were there floating there above my head. I'll ask the polling workers if it was against procedure to have someone deliver me a pizza.

Interest will be at fever pitch as the seconds tick down. Every major network will be waiting outside to hear from how the last undecided voter voted.

Then with just moments to spare, I'll do what I figure by then every still-undecided voter in America will be bound to do to settle this momentous matter.

I'll flip a coin.

It'll be Election Day and it'll be tearing us apart.

Chapter 17

Death

I began to sense I was developing a ghoulish forte for writing about neighborhood deaths when a friend offered to pay in advance for a post-mortal profile. He'd just received a troubling heart diagnosis. By telling me his ticker was tanking he'd thus put me in an awkward spot. I for the first time had base financial interest in the demise of a pal.

I momentarily began to consider homicidal options. Not only would the windfall clear in one fell swoop my bar tab, the scenario might make a dandy small-town potboiler franchise.

"Murder, He Wrote!"

Happily (I guess), he pulled through, although to this day when I ask, hey, how you doing, I feel like I should carry a stethoscope to verify the vitals.

But it was disconcerting. People were digging my grave stories. I think it's because they were so irreverent. They mentioned death as the impetus for the story, but did not gloss over the human flaws of these former humans.

Fred conveyed to children it's okay to feel sad or cry.

I conveyed it's okay to … *laugh*.

I think it goes back to 2014 when Roger Ebert was criticized for a flip remark about the DUI death of a young stunt actor, igniting a debate about the propriety of speaking ill of the dead. Here's some of what I wrote:

Can't speak ill of the dead? Why the hell not? I guess it makes sense if you're spooked by ghosts. But for someone like me, uncomfortable with confrontation, I can't think of a better time to honestly address consensus flaws and shortcomings of a person than when they're no longer around to punch me.

Really, talking ill of the dead should be a lively enterprise. I'm thinking here of newspaper obits. There's no sensible reason death notices have to be so deadly dull. They read like phone directories: "Frank died. Frank worked. Frank had kids. Frank had grandkids. Frank golfed. Say goodbye to Frank at McLaughlin & Sons Funeral Home today from 3 to 5 and 7 to 9 p.m."

It practically kills me to read obituaries.

I could change all that overnight if one insightful publisher would give me free reign over what we in the newspaper business used to call the "dead beat."

My honest obituaries would be more lively than the sports pages.

"Frank, a Latrobe boozehound, died of the massive heart attack his friends had been predicting since 2007. Married and divorced three times, he was an emotionally distant husband, was mocked for his Moe Howard haircut, and was known to area waitresses as the town's worst tipper. He failed to pay child support to four children who are now dysfunctional adults nursing substance abuse problems of their own. He cheated at golf, sent annoying ALL CAPS e-mails and frequently drove in the passing lane with his left turn signal on. Frank worked at Kennametal."

And that would just be the standard disquisition. God have pity on the poor sad (child born out of wedlock) who dies owing me more than $10.

Newspaper circulations would skyrocket. What once bored would magically entertain and, best of all, everyone would be on notice they'd better start behaving -- at least those who've been informed they only have six months to live.

We need to talk ill of the dead to help the living understand there are consequences to going through life mean, petty and stupid.

We need warts 'n' all death notices that really tell it like it is.

But what do we call something so derogatory, so crass, so antithetical to polite society?

How about … "oBITCHuaries!"

I think these were embraced because mourning in a small town like Latrobe, death can become routine. Live here long enough and you know most of the people in the daily death notices.

We lament death, yes, but we simultaneously celebrate life.

And as the whole world found out with the 2016 death of Arnold Palmer, we're pretty good at it.

We may be small town, but that doesn't stop us from being big-time when it comes to proper mourning.

Life lesson on ...

Small-Town Funeral Etiquette

Latrobe is one of those small towns where the daily obituaries are crowded with friendlies, church acquaintances and kin of people who fix our cars, our furnaces, etc. Live here long enough and attending funerals becomes as ritualistic for some people as Bingo Night down at the VFW.

There was a big funeral here — it was July '11 — and the whole town turned out. The woman and her family are beloved and at 62 she died too soon. Karen will be missed.

I was talking with some friends about it earlier in the day. One man said he wasn't going to attend.

"It's going to be too crowded. I'll just send the family a ham on Monday."

I said I admired him for his indifference to both grieving convention and doctor-recommended dietary considerations regarding the leading causes of high blood pressure.

Another friend said it drove him crazy when many people sought to console him about the death of his parents by telling him they were in a better place.

"How the hell would they know?"

He's right. Murrysville may have better schools but if the NFL lockout is resolved Steeler training camp will again be here at Saint Vincent College through August and that's always a fun time to be in Latrobe.

So thoughts of proper etiquette were on my mind as we waited in the long line to pay our respects. Lucy's just 5 and I was concerned the experience might unsettle this impetuous kid. I figured I'd better lay down some Latrobe funereal ground rules.

First: don't try and stick anything up Mrs. D's nose. She's

unlikely to react the way I do when you try shoving crayons up mine when I'm sleeping, but that doesn't mean it's right.

Do not sneak behind the coffin and start shouting in your little cartoon voice, *"Help! I'm not dead yet! Get me a doctor! Help!"* Sure, it'd be funny, but it would likely offend stuffy traditionalists.

I told her not to remove from the coffin anything shiny she thought was pretty, not to pinch the body or yell, "Boo!" an inch from the deceased's ear.

The family was delighted to see me. I could tell because they immediately began to insult my hair, my sobriety and the way I was dressed. One sarcastically said it was "real classy" of me to wear a bowling shirt to his mother's funeral.

(It wasn't a bowling shirt. It was "recreational sportswear." Val talked me out of wearing an actual bowling shirt because she said it wouldn't look real classy.)

The ridicule was so intense I briefly considered faking a massive heart attack just so they'd be forced to say nice things about me in the hopes I might revive and not upstage their mom's funeral.

I did nothing of the sort. It would have been very poor funeral etiquette.

And I knew Lucy might reach for the crayons in Val's purse and jam one up my nostril. My antics would be exposed as ruse. EMTs should keep a box of Crayolas in their lifesaving kits. I swear they work better than -- *"Clear!"* -- those high-voltage defibrillators.

I'm glad I live among a people resilient enough to prevent even the saddest of occasions take the fun out f-u-n-erals. I guess I should have encouraged Lucy do her macabre ventriloquist act behind the coffin. Everyone would have had a good laugh.

I know Karen would have.

Life Lesson on ...

Dow Carnahan The Voice of Latrobe

Days like May 2016 made it impossible to maintain our pledge to always stand for silly over somber. Alas, what choice did we have? Our friend Dow Carnahan, 56, had died.

An announcer for 30 years with WCNS, the hometown AM radio station, all the obituaries are calling him "The Voice of Latrobe," which he was. He broadcast the Latrobe Wildcats high school football and basketball games and did the same duties for Saint Vincent College. He also announced racetrack competition at the area speedways. He did the news, too, and in 2013 and 2014 won the peer-awarded "Outstanding Local Radio Newscast" by the Pennsylvania Association of Broadcasters.

What I most respected about him was how little this kind, gentle man felt the need to speak. Dow was a great talker.

He was an even better listener.

The distinction is key because we live in an age when people are celebrated for relentless volubility. It's true in our politics, our celebrity and even in our small-town bar rooms.

Loud, opinionated people — even the obviously ill-informed — dominate the room.

Dow, a big lanky dude, could have been that guy. He could have been a huge blowhard. Nobody would have minded at all. But that was never his way. That was a big part of his appeal.

Back when The Pond was still The Pond and Dave Carfang was behind the bar and it was three-deep with happy guzzlers on Friday nights, Dow would often quietly saunter in after broadcasting a game down at Memorial Stadium.

You felt privileged if he came up and stood beside you for a drink. He'd share insider stuff on all the Pittsburgh teams and the big-shot broadcasters who'd befriended him.

Everyone who knew Dow liked Dow.

You can say that about a lot of people, but mostly for logistical reasons. Most people don't know many other people.

Dow knew everyone in Latrobe and everyone in Latrobe liked Dow.

Again, this is a rare feat in a small town where youth sports are so dominant. This is the kind of town where sports editors for the local paper have been punched in the nose for not being sufficiently boosterish.

Dow covered controversies, but he was never controversial. Not once.

A friend of mine messaged me Saturday morning that Dow died in a movie theater Friday evening. I and the rest of the local irreverents have been eager ever since to learn which movie killed him off.

He was alone (his long-time girlfriend had died in August) and when the movie ended, staffers thought he'd fallen asleep and tried to rouse him.

They failed.

To me, it's a Hall of Fame death and an aspirational way to go.

I'm proud to say I'd been a guest on his popular Saturday morning talk show.

He said he'd taken "Use All The Crayons!" on a Mexican vacation so magnificently relaxing he spilled a pink drink on the pages. He showed it to me.

The tipsy desecration made me happy.

He said he loved the book and was going to apply the tips, one of which makes me feel slightly uneasy in the wake of his situational death:

"153: See a movie solo. It feels very liberating."

It's odd how some population decreases have a way of making some small towns feel bigger, less personal.

With Dow's death, our communal identity is diminished. We're no longer who we were. His quiet passing, so much like his life, seems imbued with unspoken grace and dignity.

Just like Dow.

I'm already missing him so much.

So today, please, share a moment of silence for the passing of a beloved man gone too soon.

We'll all miss that rare gentleman who could be as eloquent in all he said as in all he left unsaid.

Life Lesson on ...

Excessive Mourning

Being alive in a small town means you spend a substantial amount of time mourning those who suddenly or otherwise no longer are. You attend a lot of funerals. Each is compelling and sad in its own way so I'm often drawn to write about them.

This can be tricky. I don't want to say anything rude or be less than honest memorializing, say, a beloved town drunk.

And you don't want to by omission snub someone by ignoring their passing, but I worry saluting so many would be unwise. The topic might become maudlin for Midwest readers who enjoy reading about things like the day the barnstorming troupe of gypsy strippers showed up at the Tin Lizzy.

But the passing of Susan Sniezek, 69, is too momentous to ignore. I loved her very much. Everyone did. And we love Marty, her husband of 50 years, and their daughter, Jenn, and her wonderful family.

They're just these incredibly warm and funny people, the kind when as soon as you walk away from seeing them you immediately begin looking forward to the next time you get to see them.

Now, none of us will ever see Sue again.

But, I swear, none of us will ever forget her.

I could tell stories all day, but because of my stated fears of the blog becoming stale, I promise I'll only mention her name once more and it won't be until the very end. And instead of death, we'll talk about life.

Because on the very day our friend died, a baby girl was born in the same hospital. Her parents named her Rachel. Here's some rosy speculation of how Rachel's life could go if she turns out blessed the way few are.

Her parents will be wise and loving. She will be raised with a spirit of playful adventure. As a youth, she will travel to places like Norway where she will dance and sing so exuberantly on public transportation that even work-weary Norwegian commuters will be cheered by the youthful Yanks.

She will meet a young veteran who drives an ice cream truck and woos her with free treats. It will be the beginning of a more than 50-year romance so vivacious it will inspire countless young couples that a marriage like theirs is worthy of emulation.

Their marriage will involve enduring joy that will brighten memories and unbidden heartbreak that will bestow soulful compassion for those who grieve.

She'll be the kind of mother who lets expectant mothers see that raising a sweet, beautiful daughter — and every single daughter is somehow sweet and beautiful — is life's greatest joy.

Rachel will engage in an active and euphoric social life and when the bar door swings opens and people see her blond hair and smiling face walk in all will be more glad they decided to visit the club on that day.

Heck, all will be more glad to be alive.

She'll be the kind of parent who never misses her daughter's activities and audibly cheers her on and only slightly less audibly cheers on all the other kids.

From both teams.

Other people will throw fine seasonal parties. For Rachel and her dear husband, the parties will never end. They will turn their spacious basement into a lively saloon where all will be welcome.

Maybe they'll call it, oh, the "Neon Moon."

She'll never outgrow her sweetly childish love for Christmas and will festoon her home with more than 600 Santa Claus holiday knickknacks. By doing so, she'll let everyone know it's okay to be a kid again at Christmas, and all year-round, really.

And when news spreads around this small town that Rachel

is sick, the whole town will say fervent prayers that God intervene because towns like this need our Rachels.

And, hallelujah, God will listen.

And one day many blessed years later some old men will be sitting on a park bench and maybe see Rachel pushing a stroller with her adored granddaughter.

"Well, here comes Rachel," one might say to the other. "Isn't she beautiful. Loved by men, admired by women, resented by none, hers is a light that illuminates the whole world, the kind that will never truly die."

"Yep, she's one of the kindest, most generous and sweetest people I've ever known. Truly, 1-in-a-million."

"More like 1-in-100-million."

"Reminds me of Sue Sniezek."

Life Lesson on ...

Death of the World's Most Cheerful Man

I've lately been waking up angry Dick Guenther taught me to drive when I was 16. I wish Dick Guenther hadn't taught me to drive until I was 50.

I was thinking this as I was listening to loved ones memorialize this truly great man on Saturday at Christ United Methodist Church in Bethel Park near his Castle Shannon home.

See, I was just so stupid when I was 16. Stubborn, selfish, sass-prone — and those are just the character flaws that begin with the letter "s."

Val asked me why my own old man didn't teach me that rite of passage. I don't know. Maybe Dad didn't have the patience, thought we'd clash or maybe he didn't want the obligation to cut into his bar time.

Like father, like son!

Or maybe he wanted his impressionable young son to spend one-on-one time with one of the most kind, cheerful, generous and loving men any of us have known. Dick and his surviving wife Bernice were two of my parents' dearest friends.

Guenther, 92, was a retired postal carrier whose route included Willow Avenue in Shannon. Tony's Barber Shop was on Willow. It's where Dad used to take Eric and me for buzzcuts when we were kids.

Our visits, it seemed, always coincided with Dick's daily delivery. More than four decades later, I remember the details still.

He'd spring through the door like his blood was carbonated. He'd razz Tony, Tony'd razz back. They'd belittle Pirate pitching from the previous night's game. Some local politics would be disparaged and, boom, like that he'd be gone. You could hear him resuming his chipper whistling before the door even closed behind him. The whole conversational tornado lasted fewer than 40 seconds.

In its windy wake were smiles. I believe we can truly take soulful nourishment just by observing a happy person living their happy lives.

Guenther was the reason I became so confused when the term "going postal" began to signify workplace violence.

How could anybody who wore the same uniform as Dick Guenther ever have a bad day?

It's my understanding Guenther'd had only one bad day his entire life. He was visiting France when some strangers tried to kill him.

They were Germans. It was about a month after D-Day. Had I been there, I'd have said, "Whoa! You can't kill Dick Guenther! This war is the reason the world needs men like him. And he has so much left to do. He's going to raise three wonderful children and dote on more generations of grandchildren.

"Now, put down those weapons and let's talk this all out. Who needs a glass of lemonade?"

I hadn't seen his son, Danny, in nearly forty years. We had a good hug. He said he couldn't remember ever hearing his Dad complain about anything in his entire life.

I told him I'd found four things to complain about just crossing the church parking lot.

I'm not kidding when I say I regret he taught me to drive when I was 16. Being a bone-headed young fool, I'm sure I asked this truly great man questions about the finer points of parallel parking, proper braking distance and what to do when the lights on the stupid school bus blink red.

Had I been older, more seasoned, more aware, I'd have asked him the really important questions about just how he did it all.

How in this world of hurt and hate did he remain so cheerful? How did he make the daily joy and well-being of others his life's priority over his own? Did he ever have any idea how inspirational he was being just by being so happy?

Dick Guenther teaching a snotty 16-year-old kid how to drive just seems like a blatant squandering of a magnificent natural resource.

He's a man who could have taught the whole world how to fly.

Chapter 18

Happiness

By now we should understand it is a inexcusable disregard of proper definition — not to mention our mutual self-interest — to call "Mister Rogers' Neighborhood" a children's program. It's like calling The Gettysburg Address a stump speech; the Normandy invasion a military maneuver; the Bible a book.

It reduces something monumental to its most narrow, base description. In doing so, it strips the program of all its complexity, exaltation and grandeur.

I don't know why I'm complaining because that's exactly what Fred did with one of the most complex dynamics in the history of man: that being how one human being deals with another.

He didn't expound for marathon lectures backdropped by enormous chalk boards scrawled with indecipherable formulas. No, in a warm, simple and homey setting, he in a quiet and reassuring voice talked about the need to be kind, patient and understanding, a message he would reiterate over and over again and again.

He didn't court controversy with catchy slogans.

He never said men were from Mars, women were from Venus. He said we were both from 'round these parts and that while tension is inevitable and divorce a sad possibility, things would usually work out if everyone involved stayed down-to- earth.

He didn't fret that someone moved his cheese. He was more

concerned about everyone understanding it's wrong to move cheese or anything that doesn't belong to you and, really, isn't there enough cheese to go around so everyone could have a nibble?

You say I'm OK, you're OK? Friend, Fred would say you're more than just OK. You're special just because you're you.

He could masterfully summarize entire books, philosophies and movements with fewer than a dozen words.

• "Who you are inside is what helps you make and do everything in life."

• "Think of the ripple effect that can be created when we nourish someone. One kind empathetic word has a wonderful way of turning into many."

• "Solitude is different from loneliness, and it doesn't have to be a lonely kind of thing."

Concise and affirming, they'd all fit nicely on our refrigerator doors. And note the deliberate pithiness. No five-syllable words, no frilly sentence complications, no pretentiousness phrasing like for instance, "deliberate pithiness." Just stout batches of sound soldiers dispatched to serve authentic truths.

So calling his show a children's program unnecessarily narrows an audience to the ones too young to instigate any minor road rage. More acceptable and unique would be calling it humanity programming. That would expand the target audience to every man, woman and child on the planet and all would benefit from viewing the program the way I belatedly did.

See, I wasn't the kind of kid who'd watch Mr. Rogers when he was growing up. Instead, I watched "Scooby-Doo." So I wasn't exposed to heartwarming wisdoms about sharing, open-mindedness and the value of caring for one another. I was raised with lessons about how I and a cheesily animated, semi-literate Great Dane could ward off Egyptian Mummies, faceless zombies and — *"zoinks!"* — ghosts who'd gotten a charge out of a 10,000-volt transformer.

I know what you're thinking:

"Ruh-Ro!"

I don't think it warped me. I never (rarely) did drugs, avoided strong spirits (until the beer ran out), and displayed a strong work ethic (until the boss turned his or her back). I wasn't a bad guy.

It's just that I was never a very good one.

And it wasn't until I began watching Mister Rogers with my daughters on my lap, I realized I had the potential to become a great one.

Everyone does.

The lessons of Fred Rogers don't come with any sell-by date. They are as vital today as they were 50 years ago and will remain relevant 150 years from now.

Is Latrobe special? I asked others that question earlier in this book. I ask it of myself here.

Yes, Latrobe is special. It's special because this will forever be known as the birthplace of one of history's best and most loving role models outside of Bethlehem.

When our sons and daughters are 3 to 6 years old, we feel a communal obligation to sit them on our laps and have them watch the show starring the man who lived right down the street. Remember, we tell them, that statue by the fountain, the one of the man with the kind, smiling face you were playing on last week? Well, here he is!

There' s a reason town leaders pay men and women like Jon Hair, Karen Howell and Robert Berks to create statues of famous native sons and daughters. They don't do it so we'll remember what they looked like. No, they do it so we'll remember their values. Because those are the values we want our towns to embody.

It's why it's unlikely the town of Haifa, Israel, will ever unveil a statue of KISS founder and native son Gene Simmons.

I've claimed I was born here because it was in Latrobe where the clay of my personality was formed by men like Ned Nakles Sr. and The Snapper. If you accept that analogy, then consider I was baptized by the Rev. Fred Rogers.

Watching the show with my children had a profound and

enduring impact on me. I learned not only was I special (in Fred's eyes, we all are), but that I could be better, do better. And for the sake of our children, I ought to at least give it a shot.

Truly, I never appreciated that most of us are not born with characteristics like honesty, virtue, integrity and humility. Unlike inherent height/complexion/eye color and other appearance genes, those individual nobilities are not preordained. In fact, they're not traits.

They are decisions. We teach those values in our schools and churches, but none of the students are under any obligation to adopt them and live up to their meanings. The grade you get in gym will have more impact on your academic compass.

After about three years of watching Mister Rogers I decided I was going to at least try to become a great man. I was going to attempt to become a worthy role model and, hallelujah, there is some tangible evidence I've succeeded.

But first and in the interest of full disclosure I really ought to catalogue the ways in which I've failed. To not do so would be to risk being run out of town as a presumptuous faker.

First of all, I drink too much. I contend I spend a lot of time in bars because I'm a gregarious person stuck in a solitary job — one that out of happy coincidence happens to be in a building directly above three great bars. It's not so much I like to drink, but I've always enjoyed the rowdy company of those who do. And I can't very well sit there and sip water for 4 or 5 hours while my bar mates are paying for beers. That would be loitering and there are laws against that, laws that under some extreme circumstances lead to me in solitary confinement, again, thirsting for conversation. Who needs that?

To be fair, I don't drink as much as people think or as much as I'd like to. And I'm not as bad as my hero, Winston Churchill, to me the most interesting man since Jesus. It was said Churchill didn't draw a sober breath after the age of 40. Master Churchill biographer William Manchester said, "He was not often fully drunk, but he was never not even once fully sober."

Churchill lived to be 97 and before he died boasted the only exercise he got came from lugging the caskets of younger vegetarians and teetotalers to their graves.

It's wrong of me, I know, but it's not uncommon for me to miss dinner without informing my wife. That's a long way from greatness. But people know I like to drink in The Tin Lizzy and some of them drive a long way to sit and drink and tell me their stories. Time gets away from me and I infuriate my wife by missing dinner without so much as the courtesy of a phone call or text.

It's terrible, I know.

What's odd to me is I know at that very moment my wife is thinking of how to best dismember me, there is a car full of new friends departing the Tin Lizzy and saying, "Man, that Rodell is one great guy. It's like he had all the time in the world for us. If he treats us, relative strangers, like that, just imagine what great father and husband he must be!"

I guess I'm a lucky man because the people who say they like me actually do like me and the people who say they love me grudgingly tolerate all my bullcrap.

I lose points on the great man scale out of what others refer to as sheer laziness. I call it strategic laziness and I deploy it any time I scheme to get out of work I consider unnecessary or otherwise stupid. It's a combination that involves one part reasoning, one part resentment and three parts delay, delay, delay. It sounds easier than it is. Ironically, avoiding hard work is hard work. For instance, I don't see any point in living in the woods and waging war on nature. So while others in the spring mow their lawns two or even three times a week, I cut mine once every three weeks or when the girls complain they can no longer locate the dog in the shag. Rather than cut the grass, I'd prefer to read a book, or watch an old cowboy movie or fool around with the missus. See, I think ours is a beautiful family residing in a beautiful home. Why mess with perfection?

My worst trait? I'm an appalling provider. I get that from my old man. He was always broke. He died as he'd lived, right on the razor's edge of insolvency. He had $219 in his savings account; $312 in checking. He left his loved ones not a dime of life insurance. The red pin on the fuel gauge of his leased Dodge Neon was hard on empty. He died broke. Lots of fathers pull that off

The trick is to die, like my father, broke *and* loved. I never resented him for not having money. Sure, he'd have been even more fun with some stable scratch. But his being broke didn't impinge on my having fun or getting the jobs that helped me pay off my college loans.

One of my problems is people whose opinions I respect the most — professors, mentors, esteemed colleagues — have always told me my writing would lead to great things. Well, so far my writing has left me with even less money than when I started.

You know what? I still believe in those who believe in me. I still wake up every day convinced something great is going to happen to me and my career. And I've said that every day since, gulp, 1992. I'm like other fathers in that I tell my daughters, "There's nothing I wouldn't do for you …" I'm unlike all of them in that I'm the only one who adds, "… 'cept get a real job."

So those are a few of the dominant flaws.

Oh, and my male pattern baldness seems to be accelerating.

For some pathetic reason the encroaching baldness troubles me the most.

What about the flip side? What evidence is there that I've become a better man by absorbing lessons from watching Mister Rogers? Is the world even a marginally better place because I've strode upon it? What good am I?

For starters, it's been more than three decades since I spent a night in jail. That's an awful lot of law abiding for a poor man (see next "Life Lesson … "Doin' Time")..

And I devoted much of that carefree liberty to being a Dad, a role people tell me I'm good at. I even have a "WORLD'S BEST DAD!" coffee mug to ratify the praise. But it'll be impossible to tell what kind of father I've been until about the year 2032. By then, my darlings will either be functioning adults or sub-functioning layabouts who contribute little to the greater good in the way of tangible productivity.

Like their old man!

I guess Exhibit A is I wrote a book that's about how to be cheerful and upbeat even when life is kicking your, er, butt. It includes 1,001 tips and 57 essays. I'm tempted to list ones readers have declared as their favorites, but I'm leery of including anything that would resemble a crass sales pitch.

I'll instead present what to me is the most important message in the book, important enough to put on page 1 under the bold-faced headline, "This Book is Free."

The first paragraph says it's free to anyone who is struggling or in the military. It lists my e-mail address and phone number. Then it says:

"The author doesn't believe a book that, at its heart, aims to help people be happy should be withheld from anyone over a few dollars. 'It's said the best things in life—love, friendship, laughter—are free,' he says. 'I don't presume this book is among the best things in life but, by God, there's nothing to say it can't keep good company.'"

I've since donated more than 500 free copies to requesting individuals from all over the country. Even paid for the postage. I don't think I'd have ever conceived of that kind of altruism had I not been moved by watching Fred Rogers.

His ripples continue ever outward, as do ours. I'll never forget the Illinois stranger who called one Christmas and said she wanted to buy 30 copies. Wow, I said, you have 30 friends? "No," she said, "I only have 10 friends, but I want to take the other 20 copies down to a local cancer ward where I know they'll do the most good."

That's great!

But am I?

I'm better than I was and, I swear, that's thanks to Fred Rogers and the people here in Mister Rogers' neighborhood.

Great? That's a steep hill for a guy prone to so much strategic laziness.

Rather than great, I'm more apt to describe myself as cheerful, optimistic, blessed, proud, persistent, eager, buoyant, content and maybe a dozen or so other words that imply happiness.

So not great. Better than that.

Grateful.

Life Lesson on ...

Doin' Time

It was only a $15 parking ticket. It had been issued to me on July 3 outside the local public library for parking on the wrong side of the road. Many would have just paid it.

Not me. It didn't seem fair. There was no sign. It was a holiday weekend on a road between a church and a small town library where my wife had asked me to pick up some books for the kids.

The only way my mission could have been more wholesome was if I'd paused to donate a spare kidney to some needy orphan.

So I took it to the local police chief. We'd never met, but have mutual friends. He looked at the ticket, looked at me, smiled and said, "Let's let this go with a warning, okay?"

Okay!

I don't know why I felt so good, but I had to fight the urge to jump up and click my heels together. It continued a run of friendly run-ins with badge-bearing folks from whom I used to instinctively run.

I've also become friendly with a Pennsylvania State Trooper whom I'd met at a golf function. We hit it off and I invited him down to my local tavern where he proceeded to make as loud an ass out of himself as those of us who don't carry loaded weapons for a living.

We all had a swell time. At the end of the night, he threw an arm around me and shoved his business card in my shirt pocket. I didn't examine it until the next day. On the back, he'd written: "Chris is a personal friend/golf buddy. Any professional courtesy appreciated."

I had to practically rub the Twilight Zone out of my booze-reddened eyes. It was a get out of jail free card!

And it's just such a sad pity that I can't think of a single circumstance where I'll ever get to use it.

I don't know how it happened, but all the menace of my youth has gradually leaked away. What remains couldn't make a decent puddle. Somehow I've become good and it seems like such a waste.

Where were these powerful friendships during my hell-raising youth? Where were they when I could have really used them?

Like the night I killed my wife.

It was 1987. All the old gang from college was in town and that meant lots of drinking. Inevitably, things got out of hand and one of my buddies, a Cincinnati lad, got busted for drunk and disorderly behavior.

The haze of history, not to mention multiple Ouzo shooters, fogs the details. I think it was an ill-advised game of toss involving empty beer bottles and a nervous valet, but I clearly remember a big steroid stallion of a cop rudely shoving him in the back of the cruiser.

As I was the semi-sober host, I felt honor-bound to take charge. I asked the officer when I could collect the miscreant.

"He's with us," was all he said.

"I understand that sir, but when, pray tell, can I come retrieve him?"

We went through a variation of this verbal minuet two more times before he growled, 'Say one more word and you're goin' with him!"

You can beat me senseless and throw my shattered body in a dark dungeon until time runs out. But no one will ever incarcerate my inner smart ass.

I said, "Well . . ."

The very next instant began a lifelong appreciation for the sturdy construction of a well-built American vehicle. He grabbed the back of my head and slammed my chin into the cruiser's hood.

I'm convinced if had been one of those mid-80's foreign cars, the force would have collapsed the vehicle and the three of us would have had to perp walk a mile to the two-cell station.

Cell one was occupied by a surly-looking punk. He never even glanced up as they threw the two of us into the cell next door.

I confess I wasn't unhappy about being there. I didn't want to go through life without having to endure some imprisonment, if for no other reason than I could feel a kind of kinship with Nelson Mandela.

After about an hour of cellmate giggling -- and it was *just* giggling -- my buddy broke the ice with unseen Prisoner No. 000001.

He said he was in for a bar brawl, drunk and disorderly. "You guys?" he asked.

"Same thing, D&D," said my buddy, a fast learner already hip to jailhouse lingo.

"You?" he asked me.

"I killed my wife."

"You what!"

"Yep. Killed her dead."

Maybe it was still the drunk part of his D&D, but I was surprised to learn he was such a sensitive sort. He was floored and came alive with interest. He asked what made me do it.

"Caught her in bed with a black guy," I said.

"Oh, man!"

"Well, she's black, too," I explained.

He asked what I did.

"Shot her right in the (rear end)," I said.

"You sure you killed her?"

"I think so. It's all so confused. All I remember is her rubbing her (rear end) and hollerin' at me."

I've heard stories of men who endure long incarceration. They say they remember the forlorness, the estrangement.

Me, I'll always remember my buddy trying to stifle all his belly laughs as I spun one of my greatest stories ever, one rich with sordid detail about my criminal life as an outlaw youth.

When they let the two of us go at dawn, we walked past our cell neighbor. He didn't even look up, too fearful to even fathom an evil so malevolent, so near.

I wonder if even one of Mandela's nights over 27 years of bitter imprisonment was as much fun as my 12 hours.

I doubt it.

He probably ran with the wrong crowd.

Life Lesson on ...

Time

It was toward the end of the family birthday festivities when Josie, 16, observed that, man, 54, is getting up there. This was in 2017.

Understand, she wasn't being at all snarky or mean. She's not that kind of kid.

I think it was more a reflection on mortality and the realization the number of years I have ahead of me are fewer than the number I have behind. I thought about her comment and brought it up the next morning as I was driving her to school.

"You were right about 54 being old, but you were mistaken about one crucial point," I said. "I'm not 54. I'm 100."

Years are convenient, but poor ways to gauge life.

I'm now 56 years old, but I've lived so much more.

It's why I told my wife on our 20th anniversary it felt more like 40 years. Do not mistake that for a slam. Not at all. Our situations have bestowed us with more togetherness than many busy working couples can justify.

We share common interests and enjoy being together — just us or with the kids. For many, many years we had lunch together every day and dinner most nights.

You can be married for 50 years but only be together for five.

My own parents for example were married for 46 years, but by my gauge were only together about 18 years, about half of them during the four years before Dad died when they were actually together a good bit and seemed to enjoy one another's company. Once they became empty nesters, they began sleeping in separate beds.

I sleep slammed up against Val all night, the sole exception being nights when our rat-like yip dog burrows in between us and leaves me sleeplessly fearful this'll be the night he decides he wants to begin nibbling on my nuts.

As for being a Dad, geez, the only time I'm not there being their father is when they're in school. We're together all the time.

It'd be impossible to underestimate the years I've logged being buddies with so many friends on golf courses, in saloons and at ballgames. The memory catalogues are thick as old big city phone books.

I'm at an age when many friends are contemplating retiring. And therein lies the rub.

They've worked — truly worked — many, many years.

I've worked about three.

It's been unintentional, for sure. Who in their right mind would plan for their entire career to be one long sabbatical? It's utterly preposterous.

I feel in many ways like an intern with a promising future. Put me in, coach.

It's like if Roger Goodell suspended Tom Brady for four regular season games so the QB's body would be rested and his vital game reactions wouldn't peak until the 4th quarter of the Super Bowl.

Not that that would ever happen.

So, you see, time is elastic and measuring your life in brute years is pure folly.

Really, the only time years are an accurate unit of life's measure is when you've been convicted of a felony and the judge sentences you to a bunch of them without parole.

Fear not death.

Fear instead the death-bed realization that you never really lived.

Insinuate yourself into enough hearts and you won't just live to be 100.

You'll live forever.

Chapter 19

Being Diagnosed with an Incurable Disease

So, okay, I have Parkinson's.

How many of you, my friends, are confused by the admission? Parkinson's? Parkinson's what? Parkinson's galoshes? Parkinson's kite? Parkinson's fruit salad?

No. I have Parkinson's Disease. So do more than 1 million men mostly and women in America. The average age onset is 60.

I am 56.

I first began noticing the unsettling symptoms in October 2015 when the left side of my body seemed to begin shutting down. My left arm would hang like a deli-window salami at my side. A slight limp began to develop as my left foot disobediently dragged.

Always a crackerjack typist, crisp keyboard strokes became tentative and at times impossible. The fingers on my left hand refused to obey cranial commands that had until recently been split-second instinctive.

Doctors couldn't figure out what was wrong. So on a miserable day in early February 2018, I was given the miserable task of having to drive to Pittsburgh's UPMC Hospital to undergo a $10,000 DAP test that involved injecting me with nuclear isotopes that would circulate throughout my brain.

And on Valentine's Day, just before lunch, all alone in my shabby little office, I found out in the most graceless way possible I was one of 60,000 Americans each year who learn we have this progressive neurological disorder that in its most severe cases can rob victims of even the most basic motor skills right down to the ability to blink one's eye.

My grim informant had no time for blow-softening small talk: "Well, your test results came back and are consistent with Parkinson's Disease. There is no cure."

I went quiet so long she must have thought I'd either dropped the phone or dropped dead.

"You still there?"

I mumbled confirmation. What could I expect was going to happen?

"Can you still feed yourself?"

I told her I'd managed to down a donut that morning, but that some of the rainbow sprinkles fell on my lap. Will the inability to swallow strike by lunch?

"Well, you should really talk to the doctor."

I told her I couldn't believe the doctor, whom I've come to like, would outsource such a sensitive phone call to someone so clearly insensitive.

Note: it's not Parkinson's Condition, Parkinson's Malady or Parkinson's Inconvenience; It's Parkinson's Disease. So semantically at least this is some serious, er, stuff. Doctors have told me they have patients in their 70s who with treatment display no visible symptoms. They tell me my relative fitness and otherwise sunny disposition mean I'm a good candidate for a rosy eventuality.

But seared into my memory is a conversation with an old neighbor from the street where I was raised. We golf together once a year and a couple of years ago I introduced him to Arnold Palmer. It was the first time I think he looked at me and didn't see a runny-nosed kid riding his Big Wheel.

I treasure his friendship.

It was about four years ago he confided in me his sweet wife of 35 years had been diagnosed with Parkinson's. We talked about it for a compelling 30 minutes and to this day all I remember him saying are two words with dreadful conviction as he drilled me with his eyes.

"It's horrible … horrible."

She's in dire straits — and, no, not the cool one where Mark Knopfler, one of my very favorite performers, sings and plays peerless guitar.

Coincidentally, it was Dire Straits who in 1982 released a song that contains the only mention of any Parkinson I've ever heard or known of. It's on "Industrial Disease," a catchy number about unregulated factory ailment and what it can do to a man. Pertinent lyrics:

"Dr. Parkinson declared: 'I'm not surprised to find you here
You've got smoker's cough from smoking, brewer's droop from drinking beer
I don't know how you've come to get those Bette Davis knees
But worst of all, young man, you've got Industrial Disease!'"

I wonder if the victim maintains the ability to blink.

In fact, the disease was named for London physician James Parkinson who in 1817 begun groundbreaking research into what since AD 175 had been known as "shaking palsy."

I don't yet do much shaking. My left arm — I thank God it's, so far, not my dominant right side — shakes when it's cold, when I use it to lift plates into a cupboard or when it's under stress. Sometimes when I'm nervous and giving a speech it begins to shake so I put my hand in my pocket to conceal the quiver. It's not a good look, but I wouldn't want the shaking to distract from what I'm trying to say.

I wonder if in five years I'll read that last sentence and marvel at my quaint innocence.

"… horrible … horrible."

Right now the limp is the worst. I walk like a man who looks like a man who with every desperate step appears to be trying to walk like a man.

It's been an embarrassment for about the last year. People look and wonder, geez, what the hell's wrong with that guy? Maybe I should begin to gauge their cool by telling them it's "Industrial Disease" and see who gets it.

I keep trying to find a silver lining and the only one I can think of is that soon this inability to blink means I'll be able to really give 'em all hell in the staring contests.

Why me, I ask.

Did I have this coming? Did I ever make fun of someone with a disability? Is this karma circling back to kick my ass?

I didn't tell my little darlings, ages 17 and 12, until Sunday afternoon. It was not easy. I love them so much and dread the reality that one of the most difficult aspects of their lives may one day involve caring for me.

I told them about the symptoms, the treatments and prognosis and said if they ever noticed me stumbling coming home from the bar late at night it wasn't because Daddy was drunk. It was because Daddy has Parkinson's.

Amazingly, they bought it.

Well, not Val.

Because of rampant infant mortality, the average life expectancy of a male born in America in 1850 was a measly 38.5 years. And that was before a single Civil War bullet was fired in hostility.

I think many people view me as youthful or, well, maybe juvenile is a better word.

But, c'mon, 56 is pretty old. Some decrepitude is inevitable. And for five decades I've had a really great body — and I don't mean that the way a swimsuit model does. I had a strapping healthy body for all the meaty years when having a healthy body is a real boon for a young man eager to have raucous fun.

I think about my body and its first 50 years the way many of you feel about that old jalopy you had in college: high mileage, low maintenance. It never needed an oil change, was great in the snow and was nimble enough to parallel park between a Mercedes and a Cadillac with both owners obsessively watching. You'd need two hands to count the number of times you'd run it into the trees and it miraculously seemed like it'd bounced right off without a a scratch.

My body climbed mountains and skied down them. It was agile enough to on the very same night run from police and chase girls. It ate like Elvis, jumped out of planes, wrestled alligators and partied so hard and irresponsibly it birthed drinking legends that among sober witnesses endure to this day.

In many ways, it's not surprising that a body that's been through all that is breaking down at 56. What's surprising is it ever made it past 38.5.

Why me?

Really, with the joyful and rambunctious life I've led, it's fair to ask, "Why not me?"

For me, the most confounding aspect of all this is professional, a surprise result for someone who since 1992 has wallowed in being utterly unprofessional. But this is not the way this story is supposed to end.

"… horrible … horrible"

Here's what Fred said that could apply: "There is no normal life that is free of pain. It's the very wrestling with our problems that can be impetus for our growth."

I concur.

I simply cannot abide an unhappy ending and I don't intend for this to be one of them. I'm already being diligent about exercise and other recommended behaviors. It's all a reminder how our happy little lives can be taken away in the blink of an eye.

But not if we cease to blink!

See, I knew there'd be a silver lining in there somewhere.

Life Lesson on ...

Latrobe's best hugger

That so many women are popping up out of nowhere to give me long soulful hugs makes me glad I last week didn't reveal I have leprosy.

If I've learned anything from the time spent since I declared I have Parkinson's Disease it's that it feels good to tell people you're not well. They tell you they're going to pray for you, offer rides and household assistance and just hug the heck out of you.

I think that's one of the great aspects of living in Mister Rogers' Neighborhood. We put aside our differences and come together to lift those who are down. I just never dreamed I'd become the one whose neighbors felt needed hugs.

They've hugged me in the bar, on the sidewalk, in the grocery store, the post office — all over the place.

I'm grateful because the human hug can be very therapeutic. Studies show a daily hug can boost immunity, lower stress, increase self-esteem and reduce depression.

All hail the hug!

It can do all that and it can do something even more magical.

The hug can make you horny!

Most human intimacy begins with a simple hug, the most notable exception being the transactional intimacy with your common hooker usually proceeded by the mood-killing question, "So, how much?"

Or so I'm told.

The stormy passions that led to the conception of most of our children began with loving hugs.

I tried to put all this far, far out of my mind when I was in the plumbing fixtures aisle at the True Value hardware when I was hit with a hug so surprising I nearly dropped my new plunger.

And, oh, what a hug it was.

It was enveloping. It was supple. It was warm. It was enduring. It was Burt!

I never knew Burt could excel at hugging like that. Belching, yes. Deer-gutting, sure. Hugging, no.

How wrong I was. I'm not using his real name because I don't want to embarrass him. But for my money Burt's the best hugger in town. This bear-like man wrapped me up in his arms and literally lifted me off the ground as he whispered soul-stirring encouragement.

I've been pleased by the number of my male friends who've stepped up for quick manly hugs. Hugs are literally touching. And to have male friends old and new express such encouraging affection really moves me.

See, this remains in a part of the nation where many heterosexual men still feel awkward putting their arms around another man in a place where other men might see it.

Places like the hardware store. Get busted hugging there and, guaranteed, you'll hear three "Brokeback Mountain" jokes before the manly uncoupling.

Maybe it was what he said that made the hug seem so extra special. Because what he said to me is what in these challenging times we all need to hear.

"You're going to be all right. Stay positive. Don't give up. We're all praying for you. If you need anything — anything at all — just let me know. We'll take care of you."

Isn't that beautiful? Feel free to imagine great, big Burt saying those heartfelt words to you with his arms wrapped around your quivering torso.

That's why I felt so bad that I'd giggled hysterically throughout this whole emotional interlude. It wasn't I felt awkward or weird.

I'm mature. I'm enlightened. I'm progressive.

But I'm also about a foot shorter than Burt and his beard kept tickling my bald spot.

Life Lesson on ...

The Will to Live

My plan to engineer my own death through massive cardiac arrest has been deep sixed since I realized my heart just isn't in it. And you can't nurture a future heart attack without a whole lot of heart.

I guess this mindset is common for people who are given an unfortunate diagnosis or hit with a sudden situational forlornness. We read the fateful end game and say, no thanks, and we try and construct a tidier off-ramp.

A lovely widowed friend of mine told me all about it. She'd lost her dear husband while he was in his early 50s. It devastated her.

"Right after he died, I started smoking two packs a day. I hit the bottle every night. I was living recklessly because I wanted to die. I had no reason to live."

I realized I wasn't as committed as she'd been when she asked what other ill-advised habits I'd adopted and all I could come up with was being less fanatical about flossing my teeth.

It's true. Nearly all my life I've been a teeth-flossing fool. When I heard I have Parkinson's, I thought, "What's the point?" Unlike my friend, I wanted my death to be gastronomic in nature. And let's pause for a moment to marvel how we live in a land of such plenty that *over*-eating is a viable death option.

I figured it would take 10 years to nurse a real whopper of sufficient fatality. I'd be 65 and the worst of my symptoms would — cross your fingers — be yet to flare. So for six post-diagnosis months, it was nothing but pizza, fried chicken, ice cream and bacon! Bacon! Bacon!

Salt bad for the heart? I put salt on my cereal.

So what made me shy away from the killer diet when I thought it might have a practical application in nurturing a fatal heart attack?

Part of it is vanity. I was/am developing a pot belly and I began/am beginning to resent it. I may be suffering from a degenerative neurological disorder with the grim potential to send me to an early grave, but I want to have an open casket so people can with some shade of honesty remark that I look good for a stiff. And I'd rather that than have an open casket because my belly is too big to close the lid.

The other part is an unabashed will to live. I've been dealt an unfortunate hand — happens to many of us sooner or later — but I still revel at being among the living. I yearn to grow old or at least older with the good-natured notion that a cure is just a day away.

It's the same reasoning why so many line up to play the lottery.

Will I resume my fanatical flossing? Nah. I'm kind of done with that. I'll just floss when I feel like it.

The will to live is strong.

The will to floss, not so much.

Learning I had Parkinson's and being asked by an informed stranger if I was still capable of feeding myself was a low point in my life. Ironically, it led to numerous highs.

I've learned firsthand — first shaky hand — how if you tell people in Mister Rogers' Neighborhood you're feeling sad they'll go out of their way to cheer you up.

One buddy wants to take me to Scotland to carouse. Another well-heeled gent wants me to pick my itinerary of the top three golf courses I've always dreamed of playing. And an old friend with a deep expense account and casual ethics about how it's disbursed thinks we should roll the dice in Las Vegas.

He knows a houseful of showgirls!

And I was in June '19 the focus of on odd male custom where men who love you most and think you're going to die in, say, 5 years, gather to engage in the wanton misbehaviors that could kill you in

2 nights. I survived that college reunion weekend in Athens, Ohio, and made it home where I'm loved by even sober folk.

Lesson: people are extra nice to you when they're convinced you're not going to be around to be such a pain in the ass much longer.

Given this outpouring of concern and lush largess I've struggled to find a logical reason to tell people, sorry, I'm not dying.

Not yet. I hope.

Part of me worries that if I tell people I could be around another 15 to 20 years they'll be disappointed. And I'm sorry to disappoint people by persisting to exist.

Don't you hate when that happens?

It appears, alas, that may be my fate.

"The great misconception about Parkinson's," one doctor told me, "is when you tell people you have it they think it means you're going to die and you're going to die soon. Really, It's the best incurable disease you could wish to get."

And isn't that a perfectly charming way to convey bad news?

People ask me how I'm feeling.

"I feel like I'm living life perched atop a trapdoor with a rusty hinge."

The docs say that's a poor analogy. I say they're wrong. It's a wonderful analogy.

It's just not in my situation an apt one.

Any downturn in my condition won't be as dramatic as disappearing through the floor. It'll be gradual.

My doctors say my PD is slow progressing and that I'm high-functioning. That's good. The worst part for me is the virtual uselessness of my left hand when it comes to typing.

It's a stubborn detriment to productivity — as if I need yet another one of those.

Along those lines, some people have asked if I'm going to stop drinking alcohol.

I should note that none of these people tend bar at the Tin Lizzy where they spend their entire shifts ensuring the inebriation of me and my drunken friends, the ones who'd never dream of asking silly questions about my drinking.

In fact, I don't drink near as much as you think — or as much I'd like — but lively saloons have been my native habitat since, gee, about the 4th grade.

I excuse this habit because I tend to be a gregarious person toiling in a very solitary endeavor. Solitary that is if you don't count the 1,000 ceaseless voices raging in my head. At the end of a long day (usually about 2 p.m.) it enriches my soul to stop working and go out to be amongst the folks.

And the left hand doesn't mind pitching in when it comes to raising a glass so I count it as part of my physical therapy!

Some PT sessions did wonders for my attitude. My enthusiastic therapist says I'm in a great position to keep symptoms at bay for many years. She said my eagerness to exercise will play a pivotal role in ensuring I will have many quality days in the years ahead.

My goal is to exercise with such fervor that years from now many of you will seethe with suspicion that I faked the whole diagnosis just to get hugs, attention and free golf.

And that one of you will be so incensed you'll shoot me to death in my sleep, a much tidier demise than ones I've darkly envisioned during low points of the past year.

What can I say? You have your bucket list. I have my kick-the-bucket list.

And I hope I am deserving of any kindness you extend to me as I continue to lurch bewildered through what's left of this sweet life. I will be happy to reciprocate.

Because I intend to live for as long as I'm not dying.

Right here.

Right now. See, I'm a lucky man, likely no luckier than you. It's just that I've always realized it and it's better in some ways to be appreciative than lucky.

Chapter 20

Comparing Fred to Jesus

Fred Rogers died in 2003. Jesus Christ died in about 0032 and with the exception of glorious Easter sightings of The Savior neither's been seen since. But in some essential ways, it's like neither of them ever left.

Their messages are timeless, as evergreen as fresh Christmas trees found growing wild on winter walks. Both emphasized forgiveness, love and understanding in eras where materialism and self seemed to swamp our better intentions. So much alike. Is Mister Rogers one of the few human beings worthy of being described as Christ-like without it sounding blasphemous?

Jesus healed the sick. Fred healed hearts.

Jesus saved our souls. Fred in 1969 saved PBS.

Jesus forgave our sins. Fred forgave Eddie Murphy.

Jesus walked on water. Fred arose between 4:30 and 5:30 and went swimming naked in it just about every day for as long as he lived.

But is comparing Mister Rogers to Jesus Christ outrageous? Those who do so so do with utter sincerity and are not prone to wild exaggeration.

His holiness is a lively and engaging topic in some corners of the internet

"Mister Rogers was not just special; he was a saint. He'll never be officially offered that title, and he'd probably want it that way," wrote Jonathan Merritt, author of *Learning to Speak God from Scratch* (Convergent Books, 2018), in a November 2015 article for *The Atlantic*. "Instead, he has been canonized in the hearts of his viewers—Saint Fred, the patron saint of neighborliness."

"Fred Rogers was an ordained minister, but he was no televangelist, and he never tried to impose his beliefs on anyone. Behind the cardigans, though, was a man of deep faith. Using puppets rather than a pulpit, he preached a message of inherent worth and unconditional lovability to young viewers, encouraging them to express their emotions with honesty. The effects were darn near supernatural."

An insightful January 2018 *Washington Post* piece by Tyler Huckabee said: "The news that Tom Hanks will be portraying Fred Rogers in a coming biopic was met with frenzied glee, as Hanks is one of the few contemporary celebrities who approaches Rogers's universally beloved status. But even Hanks, for all his charms, doesn't occupy the same stratosphere of Rogers's legacy of moral and spiritual importance."

Actress Lauren Tewes said when she was at her lowest point she heard what to her was "the voice of God." It was on channel 13 and it was speaking through Fred Rogers.

Tewes was addicted to cocaine for the seven years she played cruise director Julie McCoy on the charmingly dippy television show, "Love Boat" (1977-87, ABC). It was 1984 when in the depths of her despair, she was drawn to the television by the opening notes to "Mister Rogers' Neighborhood." That's all it took. It was like "God speaking to me through the instrument of Mister Rogers," she says. She's been sober ever since.

When asked by a reporter about his unwitting role in saving the actress's life, Rogers was characteristically humble: ""How could a simple program like ours do all this? But again, the Holy Spirit can use anything."

His own son, John, said being raised by Mister Rogers was

"like having a second sort of Christ for a father," although it can be inferred his comment was less a parental compliment and more an acknowledgment of a cross he, the son, had to bear.

A now-iconic 1978 picture of a young boy cradling Mr. Rogers' face in his tiny hands and wearing an expression of pure joy audaciously hints at divinity. The photographer, Jim Judkis, worked for Rogers from that very day through Rogers' death in 2003. Judkis's daughter Maura wrote the story of the picture for The *Washington Post* in 2003. The father described the moment: "This boy immediately went right up to him and held out his hands to touch him, and he said '*Mister Rogers!*' In total awe. *Total* awe. And that was the moment of the photo," said Judkis. "I think it shows the pure attraction, the love ... it's like he's seeing God, touching God. In my opinion, Fred is close to a saint," he said.

So is the comparison warranted or is it the gulf between us sinners and the holy role model so vast that we fail to appreciate when a fellow human strives to come close?

Local clergy were asked to weigh in and relate how if having such a saintly neighbor made things easier for them.

"We're all called to be more Christ-like," says Tom Kennedy, senior pastor at Latrobe United Methodist Church. "Each of us is called to do better. That's a commitment Fred Rogers took very seriously. I struggle with the idea that any one of us can be worthy of being called Christ-like. But he was one of the few men who carried himself in way that invited the comparison. He was always striving to become more like the Savior."

His example rubs off on the civic-minded people of Latrobe, Kennedy says. "I've never served in a place where people are so willing to serve — and I truly believe it's because of him."

Martin Luther taught that we need to be "Little Christs" to one another. That was the Fred Rogers way of life says Pastor Sarah Rossing of the Saint James Lutheran Church in Youngstown (It's where our family worships and where Val plays the organ with great passion).

"Being a little Christ means to live out our baptismal promises through His teachings," she says. "That's something Fred truly embodied and did more consistently than all but a few ever have."

Another Christ-like trait was to communicate with what she calls "Quiet Courage." We live in an era, she says, where the loudest voice often, right or wrong, persuades the most people. That's not how Fred succeeded.

"He succeeded by saying simple and affirmative things quietly, but over and over again and again."

His most famous lines — "Won't you be my neighbor?" "You Are My Friend, You Are Special" and "It's a Beautiful Day in the Neighborhood" — became famous because they are positive, they're simple and he said them throughout his life.

Jesus did the same thing with profoundly similar and similarly simple lines like "Love thy neighbor as yourself."

"Fred was all about the quality of the words, not the volume," Rossing says. "And in his quiet voice you could still hear a conviction and faith that is still inspiring."

Rev. Clark Kerr recently retired from Latrobe Presbyterian Church. That was where the Rogers family worshiped and the pews to which Fred and Joanne returned when they were back in Latrobe. Kerr said he'd never call anyone Christlike because of the earthly burdens that come with the description.

"It's not right to compare the divine with the human," he says. "He was already under incredible pressures just every day living up to being Fred Roger. I think, too, that contributed to a sort of melancholy streak he seemed to have. I think it's because he was touched more deeply by life than most people. That said, I do think Jesus would have smiled at the life of Fred Rogers."

Kerr recalls The Parable of The Talents when speculating about how he thinks the life of Fred Rogers should be put in perspective. Talents, in this case, were Biblical equivalents of wealth. Before departing on a journey, the master divides up his wealth among his servants to see who ears the biggest return.

The parable is seen as Jesus's way of urging His followers to use the gifts bestowed by God in ways that will most multiply the gifts and, hence, the glories to God.

"The master says, 'Well done, good and faithful servant,' and invites him into the joy of the master."

Joanne Rogers has told interviewers that calling her late husband "Christ-like" in a way diminishes all he achieved. "Treating him like a saint keeps him two-dimensional," she's said. "His mission was to tell us that we all struggle, and he doesn't exist on another plane."

She's right. It's a lot to ask of mere mortals to emulate the Son of God.

Maybe that's why God made men like Fred.

Or maybe the problem isn't comparing Fred to Jesus. Maybe the real problem is so few of us are ever even worthy enough to invite the comparison.

Life Lesson on ...

J-Students Quizzing Christ

I taught creative non-fiction at Point Park University in Pittsburgh from 2007-2010. I felt it was then my duty to singlehandedly save journalism from boring the rest of us to death.

I realized the future of journalism was at stake when I asked the class to conduct Q&As with someone interesting in their lives, someone capable of drawing compelling attention from strangers

The results made me furious.

They asked self-centered friends what makes them cool, why their hair always looks so fabulous and how they overcome hangovers.

With the exception of the kid who asked detailed questions about hangover cures, I flunked them all (some of the kid's tips actually worked).

Was this how they intended to entertain and enlighten busy news consumers? I needed to come up with way to get them to ask tough questions that will yield revealing answers.

So I decided to have them pose hypothetical questions with three celebrity subjects who've been relentlessly grilled about their personal lives and their thoughts about important issues.

The subjects?

Mick Jagger, Gwyneth Paltrow, and Jesus Christ.

For Jagger, some asked what his grandchildren call him and if he ever makes fun of Keith Richard's amplified mumblings behind his back.

They posed questions of Paltrow about her (at the time) marriage to Coldplay frontman Chris Martin, their daughter Apple, and if they had plans to name any subsequent children after tree fruit.

But it was the questions for Christ -- some playful, others seething -- that were so riveting I included a version of the drill every year. It served an educational purpose that went beyond where you're supposed to put all the commas.

Here are some of my favorites from a group I admired as a bright and creative bunch. I think they could right now give the King of Kings a better grilling that the ones scandal-plagued celebs get from well-known softballer Larry King.

Check 'em out:

- When a bell rings does an angel really get its wings?
- What is your contact information and have you been getting your messages?
- Is there a basis of severity for fulfilling prayers? I mean, is there a keyword you're looking for?
- What would Jesus do?
- What do you do for recreation in heaven?
- If you had a driver's license printed, what variation of your name would you use? What about address?
- As a bastard son, do you resent that your birth father wasn't around more?
- After your resurrection, how did you get past the stigma of, well, how do I put this gently . . . being a zombie? Is that the real reason you ascended to heaven?
- I've broken seven of the 10 commandments. What are my chances of getting into heaven?
- Will there be a time when Miss America contestants cannot use "world peace" as an answer?
- What does your business card say?
- What have you learned about choosing friends more carefully since that Judas situation?
- Who really killed Kennedy?
- Can you tell us what's at the edge of the universe?
- How did Noah handle the woodpeckers on the ark?
- Loved that whole water into wine thing. Would you like to come to a party I'm having?

- If only those who believe that you are savior can get into Heaven, then technically wouldn't Hitler go to heaven and Ghandi to hell?
- If you competed in the Olympic games, what country would you represent?
- Why do you permit so much senseless killing in your name?
- Which came first: the chicken or the egg?
- Of all the well-known public figures from the past 200 years, who best exemplifies your ideal way of life?
- How do you justify all the tragedies/natural disasters/ accidents that cause so many people to question your existence?
- What do souls look like?

I close with a recollection of what is still my favorite question to Jesus from an aspiring journalist in a professional setting.

"So, Jesus, how are things with your father?

I like how it establishes a nice, friendly rapport, while still offering the subject an opportunity to make real news.

And it's friendly enough that it doesn't put the subject on guard for all the really tough questions that are sure to come later.

Chapter 21

I Finally Meet Mr. Rogers; It Does Not Go Well

Mom begged me not to do it. I was making a huge career-wrecking mistake, she said. It would ruin my prospects for respectable work. I'd be tainted, sordid, unworthy of decent company. For God's sake, what would she say to the church ladies? It was 1992 and I was quitting my job at the *Tribune-Review* to full-time freelance for what was then the most disreputable publication in America (its reputation has since gotten worse).

"You don't understand, Mom," I explained. "The stories I get working for just a few years for *National Enquirer* will make me so much more interesting."

"But you're already interesting enough!"

She'd come to understand, as did the church ladies, who it was later revealed were longtime *Enquirer* subscribers, bless their gossip-craving little hearts.

For me, it's never been about the money. I don't care if you're rich or poor as long as you have a lively story to tell. It can involve crime, heartbreak, passion, squandered wealth — anything. Just, please, don't be boring.

I'll never forget my first *Enquirer* tryout weekend. They'd flown me and a dozen other young reporters from all over North America to their Lantana, Florida, headquarters to see who had the craftiness, wit and just the right amount of desperation to chase, capture and tell the world's very best stories.

At night they took us to a private room at The Breakers resort in fabulous Palm Beach.They'd wine and dine us and regale us with rollicking stories of outlaw journalism. It was marvelous fun.

After a week of this, each of the prospective reporters were one-by-one called into the editor's office and given a gift bag of *Enquirer* swag and a plane ticket back home. When my turn came the editor said I could stay as long as I wanted or head back home to Latrobe. But I was welcome to work for them from wherever I wanted that to be.

I stayed another two weeks then came home. I figured I'd be better off working for myself. I knew I'd one day want to take those stories and make them my own. I knew one day I'd want to become one of those peerless story tellers I've always admired.

The quest is nearing 30 years and, "Oh, the stories we could tell." That's the name of a John Sebastian country folk song about the life's pursuit of so many guitar players like him and so many writer bums like me. I first heard Jimmy Buffett perform it on his 1974 "A1A;" Tom Petty has a 1982 version that's my favorite.

So what are some of the stories I can tell?

There were so many. Over the next 10 years, I'd report on more than 1,000 of the wackiest and most outlandish stories in all America.

I remember ones about volcano tourists who survived a shower of lava when the inactive volcano upon which they were sight-seeing suddenly became active; I remember 4-year-old children driving cars off cliffs — and living! I remember suvivors of plane wrecks, train wrecks, ship wrecks and some of the oddball hobbies high-stress people enjoyed to keep from becoming nervous wrecks.

I remember the story of an Iowa farm girl who broke into a local animal shelter to retrieve a stray dog that had brightened her days as she was being treated for cancer. Enquirer headline: *"Puppy Love Turns Ailing Girl, 11, Into a Petty Thief!"*

My favorite stories were the ones that allowed me to have fun hamming it up. I've been assigned to wrestle alligators, jump out of airplanes cruising at 3,000 feet, and once laid on beds of nails and had 50 pounds of concrete placed on my chest and smashed with a sledgehammer to demonstrate the power of the mind over pain.

When *Enquirer* editors wrote, I "felt no pain," it became the only *Enquirer* fraud with which I'd ever been associated. In fact, it hurt like hell. They ran it anyway figuring it was a victimless crime and guys like me were essentially disposable.

I saw a story about a girl who was truant so often the presiding Georgia judge ordered her tethered to her mother. The poor woman was back in front of the judge just two days later wailing about cruel and unusual punishment. Being shackled to her loved one for an intense duration was driving her nuts.

Engaged at the time, I sent in a lead summarizing the story and speculating it might be compelling to try the same sentence between two people supposedly at the height of their moony-eyed love. The result: *"ENQUIRER reporter tests his mettle for marriage! 'I spent 3 days as a prisoner of love — handcuffed to my bride-to-be!'"*

The story, rife as it is with heartbreak, hope, conflict, resolution, and finally transcendent romance, ought to be a cable movie. Maybe one of these days.

I think my best story came to me after watching a cable special about the women who used to cook for Elvis Presley, then the patron saint of all things Enquirer. I remember one cook describing bringing The King (not Arnold Palmer) a pork chop sandwich and watching him tear into it and say with butter dripping down his elbows, "This is great. Bring me six more!"

I wondered what a gut-buster diet like that would do to a normal person — and, for the purposes of this story, I considered myself a normal person. My lead, just five-words long, said it all: *"Enquirer Reporter Eats Like Elvis!"*

I still have the Brenda Butler cookbook — sing it with me! — *"Are You Hungry Tonight?"* with its recipes for burgers, pork chops and, yes, fried peanut butter and nanner sandwiches. In the end, I'd gained 20-pounds in one week. I've ever since suggested Eats Like Elvis anytime an aspiring musician was looking to name a band.

The stories I could tell.

Here's one I was assigned on October 19, 1993.

It's about Fred Rogers in rehab.

To this day I marvel at the odds that I, a sensational reporter living on a street named after Fred Rogers, was in a Latrobe tavern with a buddy who'd been in rehab with Fred Rogers' son when he learned he'd be doing a story about that very topic.

Only in Latrobe!

The Enquirer's network of stealth informants had already provided detailed accounts of John Rogers, then 32, battling a cocaine addiction. Thanks to Dickie Kemp, I had some great eyewitness color. The story was solid. All we needed was a comment from Fred.

I had a trick that was a bit novel even for back then. Today, it borders on peculiar. I still use it when I feel a need to impress a source on the gravity of any pending subject.

I wrote Mr. Rogers a letter.

I told him who I was, what I was doing, where I lived, and how sorry I was that he and his family were suffering the ravages of addiction, then — as now — a societal scourge tearing apart even affluent families led by role model parents.

Even as I was typing it, I was amazed it was happening to Mr. Rogers. Truly, if it could happen to him it could happen to anyone.

I proposed he sit down for an interview with me and share his feelings and insights about what we as a nation needed to be doing to win the so-called War on Drugs. I told him it could be a first person story, "… as told to *The ENQUIRER*." It's no exaggeration to say his involvement would have vaulted the topic into the national conversation. Every editor and producer in the country scoured The Enquirer for relatable topics. A story on parents and drug abuse spearheaded by, of all people, Fred Rogers, could make a real difference.

Then I put a stamp on the envelope and dropped it in the mailbox just down from my home on Fred Rogers Way at the Youngstown Post Office. In four days, my plan was to sneak into his office and approach him with tactful, but hard questions.

In his 2018 book "The Good Neighbor," biographer Maxwell King details, with Rogers family approval, the difficulties the family had with sons John and Jim in their rebellious and experimental phases. One passage discusses the day Joanne found the boys were growing marijuana in the basement.

"Joanne was stunned, but also a little amused," King writes. "She later speculated that at least it showed some entrepreneurial energy on the boys' part. Their father was not so easygoing. 'He was furious,' says Joanne. "It was illegal, for one thing … many people would have loved to have that story out there …"

What follows are five pages of stories told in a jocular, boys-will-be boys tone about Jim and John getting high, brawling at the dinner table, sneaking across state lines to buy beer and doing the kinds of things many brothers have always dome.

King does note how the story did surface in May 1978 when People magazine published a story under the headline, "Fred Rogers Moves Into a New Neighborhood —and So Does His Rebellious Son."

It said: "Most kids rebel against their parents sooner or later. But Jim Rogers is having a harder time than other 18-year-olds telling his father to buzz off. Jim's pop is not just any Mister Rogers. He's the

Mister Rogers, for 24 years the gentle host of public TV's "Mister Rogers' Neighborhood' and a paragon of parental understanding. A freshman at his dad's alma mater, Rollins College in Florida, Jim has stopped writing to his folks or even returning their phone calls. 'He's flown the coop,' sighs his father. '... It's been painful, and it's rough on Jamie. But if we don't allow him to go off and have this time for himself, he'll never come back to the nest.'"

The story feels to me like it pulls its punches with its aw-shucks treatment of what had to be painful times for the whole family. The King bio even more so.

Who better than Fred Rogers to explain how he dealt with an issue troubling millions of bereft parents? Why be so coy?

That's what I tried to find out in 1993 when I evaded building security at WQED and made my way through the labyrinth of stairs to the open door of Fred Rogers, but not before I was diverted on my mission by an awkward chat with one of the show's characters.

I can't count the number of words spoken between me and Arnold Palmer: Five Thousand? Ten thousand? More? It was a lot. I figure I interviewed him more than 100 times over 20 years. We talked history, entertainment, supermodels — you name it. Of course, there were golf tips. I remember the time I told him I was playing golf the next day at venerable Oakmont C.C. and was seeking his suggestions on how I could get a good score. His response:

"I suggest you play someplace else."

On the other hand, I can precisely count the number of words spoken between Fred Rogers and myself.

I said 12 to him; he said 7 back to me.

Then our, perhaps, promising conversation was abruptly concluded. I was thrown out of the building ... by Mr. McFeely!

Speedy Delivery? More like "Return to Sender."

David Newell for years served two roles. He played Mr. McFeely on the air and off it was the show media contact. I ran into him as I was looking for Fred's office. He could see I was lost. An actual interview with Fred was a veritable moonshot, highly unlikely. But all I needed to do in the eyes of my editors was confirm we'd given him an opportunity to respond and I'd be off the hook.

So when Newell/McFeely asked what I was doing, I didn't dodge. The news that his friend was having family trouble clearly upset him. He told me I needed to leave and then to my surprise turned and left.

The door to Mr. Rogers' office was open. He was standing looking at some books when I knocked. When he turned to me, I said, "Sir, I'm so sorry to bother you. My name is Chris Rodell —"

He said, "Yes, I got your letter, thank you."

I'll never forget the look on his face. He was smiling, all grace and kindness. It was the face of a man who looked like he was going to be grilled, not about drug problems, but about the possible purchase of Girl Scout cookies.

I began to wonder if this might end differently than I'd thought. And it was at that precise moment I heard Mr. McFeely say "That's him!" and felt the security guard's beefy hand clamp down on my shoulder.

I looked back at Mr. Rogers. He was still smiling serenely, but made no indication he was going to intervene. It was the last time we'd be in the same building together.

The lead story on the November 16, 1993, issue of the *National Enquirer* says, "My Miracle Baby,' by Vanna White, "Acupuncture helped me get pregnant!" The "World Exclusive" — in her own words! — is accompanied by a snazzy portrait of Vanna looking lovely as ever with some lecherous-looking gent resting his ear on her belly, which with his left hand he is fondling like it's a cantaloupe he's testing for peak freshness.

Vanna, by the way, will be 63 on February 18, 2020.

Enquiring minds want to know!

Also on the front page is a story about Whoopi dumping Ted Danson for a Beverly Hills dentist, and what happened during the sad, final hours of once-promising actor River Phoenix. Then at the bottom left is a small box that features a smiling picture of the man beside a bold-faced headline that says, "TV's Mr. Rogers Secret heartache over his son's drug addiction."

Inside on page 41 is a story about the star's "secret battle to save his son from drugs." I was pleased by how sympathetic and praiseworthy the story turned out. Enquirer reporters were mostly fact-gatherers; the editors wrote the stories so it could be a surprise how the facts were presented and the stories told. One "source" (it was Dickie) said: "I used to make fun of Mr. Rogers, but now I think he's the greatest. He'd put his arm around his son (John) and you could tell he cared so much and it was so hard on him."

It talked about the mockery, the ridicule, the cruel sarcasm. And it talked about how those same mockers one-by-one approached the man so different from them and how their tough guy facades began to crumble.

"As patients came up to say hello, he was so kind. There were drunks, addicts and hookers — people you don't see in Mister Rogers' Neighborhood. But he made no judgments and talked to everybody in that same pleasant voice.

"When I spoke to him, it was better than some of the classes. I walked away feeling better about myself, like I'd turned a corner. Like I was going to make it. And that was all thanks to Mr. Rogers."

You can criticize *The Enquirer*, its tawdry existence and the shady ways the facts were obtained, but for my money, that's the very best story I've ever heard about Fred. It's practically Biblical. Jaded men and women roaming that acre of hate and to his face mocking him and how he, without ever raising his voice, confronted the bullies, won them over, then shared whispered wisdoms that made this a better world.

It's what he was known for doing with children, but seeing it applied so vividly in such a hostile setting to struggling at-risk adults -- many of whom never had a Mister Rogers' childhood -- is magnificent and vibrant proof of how his nimble message can tear down even the staunchest walls of hateful cynicism.

Really, it amazes me the Rogers promoters conceal a story they ought to trumpet. It has all the elements of an historic battle. There's conflict, an uncertain outcome, lives are at stake, as is the very future. And there is a bona fide hero risking it all to make a difference. It's like the Battle of Gettysburg scaled down to the size of a single human heart.

I only wish he'd have followed Vanna's lead and granted me a world exclusive. I think he might have made a difference and we here in Latrobe are all about making a difference.

Life Lesson on ...

Drug-Addicted Babies

A pharmaceutical giant that makes billions aggressively marketing addictive opioids — side effects may include constipation — is now aggressively marketing a drug that relieves opioid-induced constipation. Side effects do not include, apparently, an appreciation of fine irony.

I'm interested in this because I've been feeling a bit constipated myself lately.

Constipated with love!

Let me explain. Our daughters' baby years are far behind us and our grandparenting years — knock on wood — are likely distant. I miss holding babies. My babies, sure, but any old baby will do. The memories are indelible. The tiny fingers, the hot little breaths, the heart beating like a locomotive just getting ready to really roar. Holding a sleeping baby — holding the future — is magisterial. It is at once awesome and serene.

The feeling inspired me at the time to write the, for me, profound line: "Holding a sleeping baby is better than any drug."

But because I'm a real-world guy, I followed that yin line up with the following yang: "But babies wake up and become the reason many parents turn to actual drugs."

Sad, but true. While a sleeping baby can be magnificent to behold, a wide-awake one can be an incredible pain in the, er, butt. They scream for no apparent reason, vomit on freshly changed onesies and soil diapers with alarming frequency.

Many pinched parents turn to drugs. Hard drugs. Addiction is our epidemic curse. I feel heartsick for the scores of adults who fall prey to it and its strangling consequences. I feel worse for their children. Our neonatal wards are becoming crowded with babies born addicted to drugs their mothers took while they were pregnant.

But what can I do about it? My professional life's such a mess many people suspect I have to be addicted to something narcotic. It would sure explain a lot.

Val knows how I feel about these things and she had a suggestion: I should check out the baby rockers. I told her I prefer geriatric rockers like The Stones and Tom Petty.

"No," she said, "the hospital is looking for volunteers who'll help soothe babies born with addictions. You go in and they give you an addicted baby and a rocking chair. It does wonders for the baby."

Experts say the human touch is essential to helping these narcotically addled innocents heal. In many cases, the baby rockers become momentary surrogates while the mother recovers from her own addictions. I'm thinking about doing it and encourage you to do the same.

And if you don't have time for that, innovate. There's bound to be someone in your life who could use a healing hug. It could be a child, a co-worker, a neighbor or — who knows? — maybe someone who sits across from you at the dining room table.

Lesson?

It never hurts to hug. In fact, we're learning you can literally hug the hell out of people.

Side effects may include a better world.

Chapter 22

Giving a High School Commencement in Mister Rogers' REAL Neighborhood

Here's a tip about how if you're ever asked you can ensure your Latrobe high school commencement speech is a rousing success: Scare the audience with a history lesson about what experts believe to be the longest commencement address of all time then tell them you're going to do yours in 6 minutes flat and that they can all quit listening in 30 seconds 'cause that's all that's going to matter.

That's what I did in June 2019 when I was honored to be asked to give the commencement address at Latrobe's Adelphoi Ketter Charter School in Latrobe. So it's a Latrobe high school, but not the Latrobe high school.

My ego was undiminished by the distinction. I, a long-time resident of Mister Rogers' Neighborhood, was asked to address graduating students in Mister Rogers Neighborhood about their futures and what it means to be a happy, productive earthling.

It's the kind of thing they used to ask Fred Rogers to do, but Fred wasn't around.

I was.

I took this opportunity very seriously. Truly, I was honored by the invitation to take such a high-profile role before these honest achievers.

Understand, Adelphoi isn't your typical high school. The building next to the one where I was speaking is surrounded by a security fence topped with concertina wire. To graduate last night, many of these students had to overcome addiction, abuse, abandonment, multiple court proceedings and the kind of life challenges candy asses like me and other public school grads can only imagine.

And it was my job to inspire them?

Hell, they inspired me.

But I put a lot of thought into my address, presumptuously believing my words might have some impact even as I acknowledge I remember nothing that was said at my high school graduation, who the speakers were nor if I even attended.

Yet, I imagined the 40 graduates and 200 adults would hang on my every word, words that would endure through posterity. That's why I alerted them to the only words that really mattered.

I share them with you here and now because I believe they can, if applied daily with sincere vigor, can brighten the whole world. The key advice from my speech is:

"Try and do something each and every day to ensure parking at your funeral will be a real pain in the butt."

This is, in fact, item No. 42 (out of 1,001) from "Use All The Crayons!" In the book instead of the colloquial "pain in the butt," I say, "… ensure parking at your funeral will be a real bitch." I sanitized it because I knew there would be children present. Children fluent in profanity, certainly, yet children nonetheless.

Think about it. With some adjustments, the sentiment could have come straight from Fred himself.

Here's the rest of the speech, which was very well-received. One board member told me it was the best commencement speech he'd heard in the 15 years since he'd been attending.

"For as complicated as life is, a truly successful one can be deceptively simple.

It's possible for each of you to live a life that'll lead to funereal traffic jams, TV news helicopters and scores of loved ones complaining they had to park a mile away. But they were willing to do that because you mattered.

You can achieve this in ways that have nothing to do with power, money or fame.

Being ruthless or cutthroat won't help

What will? Being kind. Being cheerful. Being persistent. And when times are toughest being all three at once.

Be a happy example of a decent human being and all the very best people on the planet will be drawn to you. They'll invite you to swanky parties, fix you up with classy dates, and bring you soup when you're sick.

How do you become that person? Here's the best part: You do it by enjoying your life.

- *Be daring: Try to do at least one thing each week that will blow your hair back and allow you to scream, "Wheeeeeeee!!!"*
- *Be opportunistic: The pessimist complains about all the times they've been thrown under the bus. The optimist thinks one day he'll make a really swell bus mechanic.*
- *Be silly: Open an art gallery with nothing on the walls. Then invite people to enter and be greeted by forty guys who say nothing but, "Hi, I'm Art!"*
- *Be determined: You're going to be challenged with hard times. Follow Winston Churchill's advice: "When you're going through Hell, go faster."*

Does anyone see what I'm asking you to become? It should be obvious. I'm asking you to become … Happy!

It's the correct answer to the wrong question every adult asks every kid: What do you want to be when you grow up?

Take it from me; What do you want to be when you grow up?

You want to be happy. Adults tend to forget that.

We fail ourselves every time we equate success or wealth with happiness. One has nothing to do with the other.

Robert Louis Stevenson knew. He is the author of "Treasure Island"

and "Dr. Jekyll & Mr. Hyde," two monumental books that have withstood the test of time.

But to me the best thing he's ever written isn't a book. It's a single sentence.

"There is no duty we so much underrate as the duty of being happy."

Words to live by.

I recently received an unfortunate diagnosis that left me feeling angry and scared. But then a prevailing emotion emerged: I became thankful.

Not for what's to come, but for all that's already happened. I can't believe just how lucky I've been.

What's funny is how nothing in my life worked out the way I was sure it would when I was in your position.

I have no prestige. No influence. No monuments … No savings.

So why am I so happy? I knew early on I wouldn't need those things.

If I were to die tomorrow, all I'd have are the warm memories of a lifetime of happiness and gratitude for being the recipient of so much genuine love.

Now here at the conclusion is the time when other, more esteemed commencement speakers are telling graduates, "You only live once!"

It's bullcrap. In fact, you'll only die once. You're graced with the option to live every single day.

So may you live — truly live — for as long as you're alive.

And may parking at your funeral one day many, many years from now be for your many friends and loved ones a huge pain in the butt.

I'm not going to say I was guided by the spirit of Fred Rogers that night, but in Latrobe when you're asked to think about children and their future, you can't help but be inspired by the spirit of Fred.

Chapter 23

Trolley Magic

I was graced with the opportunity to drive the Mister Rogers' trolley through the Land of Make-Believe for about seven minutes. As there was just me and my then- 17-year-old daughter on board and Idlewild Park was otherwise empty, my official concerns were non-existent.

I didn't have to worry about a script. I was untroubled by creaky mechanics or engaging an audience. I didn't need to monitor the kid in row 4, the one with the purple shirt and the green gills, to see if he was going to heave his extra large Potato Patch fries.

So my thoughts were intent on only one aspect of the trolley's operation and I kept intoning it over and over in my mind like some crackpot prayer.

"Fly, damn you. Fly!"

Oh, that would have been the coolest thing. I was hoping I could muster the magic to leave the track, go airborne and, as WWII pilot John Gillespie Magee wrote in the epic poem *High Flight*, "slip the surly bonds of earth and dance the skies on laughter-silvered wings ... to touch the face of God!"

Touch the face of God? I'd have been jazzed to just buzz my buddies down at The Tin Lizzy.

Magee, by the the way, was an American pilot/poet serving in the Royal Canadian Air Force. He composed *High Flight* in

September 1941 and died doing what he so loved just three months later when his Spitfire collided with another plane over England. He was 19.

President Ronald Reagan in 1986 used those very same words to memorialize the seven crew members killed in the Space Shuttle Challenger disaster.

As far as I can tell this is the first time the soaring poem as ever been applied to a wingless, earth-bound trolley incapable of exceeding 4 mph. But, oh, what the hell. It was the Land of Make-Believe, it seemed like the thing to do and I doubt Fred Rogers would object.

Because my proposed mission was more ambitious than simply joy riding over the hometown tavern. Should it ever happen again and I manage to somehow slip the surly bonds, by God, I have a flight plan that will make Santa's look simple.

I'll start by flying over the library and the elementary schools because those are the places where magic incubates into blessed reality. I'll go there first because we all know how one shy, inspired child can with incorruptible faith and hidden moxie change the whole world.

I'll then fly high above the hospitals, the clinics and the drug rehab centers — all the places where those who are down need glorious reasons to look up. We'll circle some spots twice with the understanding that some of the people who are most difficult to love are some of the same people who need love most.

I'll fly over town halls, the state capitals, and up and down the corridors of power throughout Washington D.C. — all the places where today so many bitter men and women are consumed with unreasoning hatreds for those with whom they disagree. And upon each of them, I'll drop the one thing that will cause them all to smile at one another and rejoice to be alive in a land where something so unifying, something so good, is also so plentiful.

Banana splits for everyone!

I'll be towing a banner designed to encourage emotional

fence-sitters to shed the shy and experience the physical rush that comes from doing good deeds in the hopes that one day, hallelujah, being really nice becomes really normal. It'll read, "Be Defiantly Kind!"

I'll fly that magic trolley over the cities and the villages, over the nations and territories where they worship in churches, synagogues, temples, mosques and where they humbly gather on the grass at sunrise to express the simple yet euphoric joy of just being born human.

None will be excluded.

> *People, get ready*
> *There's a train a-coming*
> *You don't need no ticket*
> *You just get on board*

Yep, we're stopping by to get you, too, Curtis Mayfield!

We're going all over the world and there will be room for both the happy and the hopeless. Together we're all flying that beloved trolley straight through the front door of every home and into the heart of anyone who's forlorn or broken in body or spirit.

We will fly low enough to startle those too immersed in work to welcome any whimsy within their walls. A sad number of adults fail to realize they were born free and have somehow spent their entire lives constructing prisons around themselves. They are enslaved by their rigors, blinded to rainbows and intolerant of distracting frivolity.

They've self-incarcerated their essential humanity.

Well, we'll be bustin' the bastards out.

We want the whole world to realize there is another way, a way where walking in another person's shoes is preferable to seizing them by their throats; that both the optimist and the pessimist are correct about 50 percent of the time, but the optimist is cheerful 100 percent of the time; and that if you take the scenic route enough in the eyes of others you become the scenic route.

And then after that one long night of love, healing and magic we're coming home, home to Latrobe. Home once and for all. Home for good.

Because of all the life lessons I've learned the one that matters most is you can find peace, contentment, love, hope and happiness when you choose in your head and commit in your heart to living the Fred Rogers' way.

It's easy for some of us. It's already home and we're not going anywhere. We're staying put. We're not leaving Mister Rogers' Neighborhood.

I hope after reading these stories Mister Rogers' Neighborhood never leaves you.

Acknowledgements ...

This book was pestered into existence by legendary Pittsburgh sports writer Jim O'Brien. "The world needs a book about the real Fred Rogers and what makes him and Latrobe so special and you're the perfect guy to do it," he'd say. When I told him I didn't know Fred Rogers he countered, "But you do know Latrobe." Jim convinced me this book would be well-received and fun to do. Before I've sold a single book, he's already half right. Jim has written 29 books in his "Pittsburgh Proud" series, including the highly acclaimed trio, "*The Chief,*" "*Lambert*" and "*Franco, Rocky & Friends – It Pays to be a Good Guy.*" He is on the advisory board for the Western Pennsylvania Sports Museum at the Heinz History Center in Pittsburgh, and has been inducted into the Western Chapter of the Pennsylvania Sports Hall of Fame.

Thanks to renowned Marie McCandless for careful edits and cheerful companionship. It was Marie who gently pointed out my vast over- and mis-use of the word "renown" and it is in her honor I use it here for the very last time. Thanks to Marie's old newspaper, The Latrobe Bulletin, for steadfast support of all my projects. Thanks to my friends at The Adams-Memorial Library and members and staff at the Westmoreland Library Network for all the enthusiastic promotional opportunities.

I'm grateful to Laurie Mcginniss at Second Chapter Books, Scott Levin at Youngstown Grille, John Rusbosin and all the other independent businessmen and women who sell my books; Robyn

John for cover design. Thanks to Vinnia Alverez at iUniverse for her cheer and to Library of Congress researcher Cheryl Adams for what to me was a "Eureka!" find.

Thanks to Buck Pawloski and staff at The Tin Lizzy for always making me feel right at home, that is if my home had three lively bars full of the kind of people anyone would like to call neighbor. You, my friends, are the reason why when someone asked what I do when I'm not having fun in the sprawling Tin Lizzy, I answered, "Well, that's never happened, but if it ever does I'll just go someplace else in The Tin Lizzy."

I consider myself a lucky man in that the people who say they like me seem to actually like me, and the people who say they love me mean they tolerate all my bull crap. Know this: If I say I like you, it means I love you; and if I say I love you — Val, Josie & Lucy — it means I really, really love you. And I really, really do.

Same goes for you, Latrobe.

— 33 —

Printed in the USA
CPSIA information can be obtained
at www.ICGtesting.com
LVHW011143171223
766416LV00038B/671